Develo

MAKING ORGANIZATI

The Quest for Purpose

Cutting-edge thinking to catalyze your leadership practice

Publisher's note

Every effort has been made to ensure information contained in this publication is accurate at the time of going to press. Neither the publishers nor any of the contributors can accept responsibility for any errors or omissions, however caused, nor for any loss or damage occasioned to any person acting, or refraining from action, as a result of the material in this publication.

Users and readers of this publication may copy portions of the material for personal use, internal reports, or reports to clients provided that such articles (or portions of articles) are attributed to this publication by name, the individual contributor of the portion uses and publisher.

IEDP Ideas for Leaders Ltd
42 Moray Place, Edinburgh, EH3 6BT
www.ideasforleaders.com

in association with the Center for the Future of Organization
www.futureorg.org

Publishers:	Roland Deiser and Roddy Millar
Editor-in-Chief:	Roddy Millar
Senior Editors:	Roland Deiser and Peter Chadwick
Associate Editors:	Saar Ben-Attar (Africa)
	Suzie Lewis (Europe)
	Conrado Schlochauer (LatAm)
	Ravi Shankar (SE Asia)
Art Direction:	Nick Mortimer – nickmortimer.co.uk

WORLD LAND TRUST™   Printed by Pureprint, a Carbon Neutral® Company, on an FSC certified paper from responsible sources. The paper is Carbon Balanced with the World Land Trust, an international conservation charity who offset carbon emissions through the purchase of high conservation land value.

ISBN 978-1-91-552906-0

www.developingleadersquarterly.com

Contents

Welcome to this our 40th issue of Developing Leaders Quarterly, which is something of a milestone as well as being the first issue of 2023.

In this issue we focus on the topic of Purpose. Often when curating these issues, the editorial task of mining interesting angles on topics and shaping them to fit well with each other and having them come from an interesting range of perspectives and contributors can be a challenge. But it seems that at the moment Purpose is at the forefront of many people's minds. Every way we turned there was an intriguing suggestion or new angle we might run with – so we had the other curatorial challenge to contend with: to whittle down lots of great content to a few key pieces that provide both breadth and depth for the topic. And I am very excited with the articles we are able to offer in this issue.

We kick-off with a conversation I had with Dame Jackie Daniel, the Chief Executive of one of the UK's largest NHS health regions. Dame Jackie has come up through the ranks of the National Health Service and understands what motivates and, crucially, what disrupts the work of the employees who keep this vital but complex organization going. Her experience and insight into the role of purpose in this most purposeful of institutions, and how to nurture and foster it, is invigorating and inspiring. My co-publisher, Roland Deiser, has an equally energizing conversation with Harvard professor Ranjay Gulati, author of *Deep Purpose* which we review in our Books section too. Ranjay had an epiphany on the role of purpose that has led him to explore new practices on management practice, Roland's excellent conversation with him unpicks this and more. Roger Delves and Ralf Schneider augment these insights with their own research from an academic and consulting perspective respectively. While Sertac Yeltekin shares his personal story of pursuing more individual purpose in the world of finance – leaving a senior role in a large organization to find a very different but more purposeful one in boutique financing in Asia.

I am thrilled to have Rebecca Stephens contributing. Rebecca was the first British woman to summit Everest and has plenty other mountains under her belt too. But here she is wearing her leadership consultancy hat and takes an historical view of explorer Sir Ernest Shackleton's remarkable escape from the Antarctic pack-ice in 1917. She describes how his personal purpose coupled with a clear vision on the expedition's purpose – albeit one that changed as circumstances changed – was integral to their ultimate survival against extraordinary odds.

We also take a look at some other themes: Amy Bradley and Katherine Semler take a look at the increasing challenge of corporate burnout – and how purpose plays a part in allaying that; while Yasmina Suleyman writes on what makes millennials tick in a wonderfully researched article that draws on Intrinsic Motivation Theory and the roots of Servant Leadership – and then provides a detailed case study of how that is working out at Spotify. Marilyn Mehlmann guides us through what makes work satisfying – and the elements we need to include to assure ourselves that satisfaction is guaranteed. Prof Beliz Ülgen shares her Chair Effect theory, on how managers often change their behaviours once promoted – and suggest some simple solutions to managing this risk.

We summarize the lively RoundTable session we had following our previous issue on Curiosity. Live discussions always unearth new ideas and concepts, with the panellists sparking off each other – and so it was for this session. I have tried to capture some of the key takeaways here – but the best thing to do is join the sessions themselves. We also provide a selection of Ideas from our Ideas for Leaders site and reviews of recent books.

Don't miss out on our online events – we are running our second RoundTable panel, this time on Purpose on March 6th, and before that Rebecca Stephens is in discussion with me on Shackleton and Purpose on February 28th. You can find out more on the DLQ's online events pages – see the panel below.

Roddy Millar | Editor-in-Chief

If you have any stories you would like to share with us for potential pieces in the magazine or for discussion on the DLQ website, please let me know at **editor@dl-q.com**.

For more information and to register for a DLQ event visit:

developingleadersquarterly.com/current-events

Roddy Millar in conversation with
Dame Jackie Daniel, Chief
Executive of Newcastle-upon-Tyne
Hospitals NHS Foundation Trust

Nurturing Purpose in a Purpose-Led Organization

D ame Jackie Daniel is a purpose-led leader. This is evident not just from the intentional focus she brings to fostering and strengthening the role of purpose in her organization, but from the values she has identified in building her leadership style and approach.

Today Dame Jackie is the Chief Executive of Newcastle-up-on-Tyne Hospitals NHS Foundation Trust, one of the largest semi-autonomous organizations in Britain's National Health Service. Here she heads-up over 18,000 employees and runs a budget of £1.4billion (approx. $1.7bn). She received her Dame-hood in the Queen's New Year's Honours list in 2018 having turned around the failing University Hospitals of Morecambe Bay NHS Foundation Trust.

The 'purpose' of 'caring for people when they're at their most vulnerable' is a hugely powerful motivator, it is not a sufficient condition to just enable the smooth running of a complex healthcare organization

None of this was inevitable for her. As Jackie describes it "I crashed out of school and didn't attain the qualifications I needed, to do what I wanted to do. So, I didn't go on to university at that stage, and kind of fell into the NHS, into nursing..." and then she notes about arriving in nursing "I knew, as soon as I got there that I'd found my place and my purpose in terms of caring. Caring for patients when they're at their most vulnerable, I suppose was where it started."

The NHS remains a totemic institution in the British psyche, offering free treatment to all, at a total cost far below that spent on healthcare in many other countries , notably the US. That it sustains great care for the vast majority in spite of this underfunding is founded on the dedication and resilience of its staff at all levels, from hospital porters, through nurses to doctors and consultants. While the 'purpose' of 'caring for people when they're at their most vulnerable' is a hugely powerful motivator, it is not a sufficient condition to enable the smooth running of a complex healthcare organization such as the Newcastle-upon-Tyne hospitals that Jackie Daniel heads-up.

Dame Jackie Daniel

Wings to Fly

As she quickly rose through the nursing ranks, she observed that providing the best care, also required good leadership. And that that leadership needed to include a large amount of care too. "As soon as you get to ward manager, ward leader level, you begin to appreciate the impact that you're able to have on a ward of 30 patients... I appreciated that was largely down to leadership. And you could see the direct correlation. I've seen that at every career transition I've had, and that's driven me. I thought 'I can create an environment where people flourish, people get the best care, feel really satisfied and highly motivated about what they're doing. But what about the rest of the hospital?' And that's what led me to first become a director."

Dame Jackie uses an interesting metaphor for how she sees the organization from her CEO's perspective: that of an 'airplane'. The fuselage is the part that most chief executives

The key parts are the wings which, she explains, are the culture, the values and the behaviours of the organization, "these are the things that amplify and accelerate progress. They get you the altitude and traction through really good, aligned leadership"

focus on—the strategy, the finances, the annual objectives. The cockpit also has a range of dials and meters that allow the leader to monitor the governance and risk of those operations—something that she feels is too often under-monitored by NHS leaders with occasionally dire consequences. The key parts are the wings though, which she explains are the culture, the values and the behaviours of the organization, "these are the things that amplify and accelerate progress. They get you the altitude and traction through really good, aligned leadership" she says.

Dame Jackie received her Damehood for her work at Morecambe Bay NHS Trust. When she went there it was an organization that was catching nationwide media attention for its failures in care quality, with particular focus on deaths of mothers and babies at one particular hospital. But the care issues were widespread across the trust. It was here that Dame Jackie was confronted with the real need to mix the art and science of leadership. She has been designing her own model of lead-

ership over the years "my kind of central operating framework which is all the classic stuff around strategy, breakthrough objectives, clear values...". At Morecambe Bay not only was none of this kind of structure in place as "their strategy [had been] all about acquisition and building the business financially; and nothing actually about quality." But also "there wasn't a sense of organization, there wasn't a sense of 'team Morecambe Bay'." Without this sense of 'Morecambe Bay as an organization' there was a responsibility gap, everyone was operating as individuals and few had any clear sight of their purpose within the wider structure.

Enabling Purpose

Purpose at work may be an intangible element, but people can feel when it is present. It is part of a leader's role to foster that feeling of purpose in their staff. In Morecambe Bay the purpose that drew people to work in the caring environment

In order to ensure that the strategy flies, it is necessary to have everyone lifting it and propelling it forward. That is the real leadership challenge, that requires alignment and purpose to be held with clarity across the organization

of the NHS was not being nurtured, but rather a disconnected commercial one was leading the organization, which neither resonated with the staff nor enhanced the care being provided by the organization.

One of Dame Jackie's first actions was to clarify people's responsibilities and ensure everyone knew what other people were responsible for. Morecambe Bay operates over a large rural geography of the southern part of the English Lake District, so this was not as simple as it might seem.

In focusing on the people, she was able to bring the art side of her leadership into play. Setting the technical, science side was simpler—writing the strategy and setting the objectives, but Jackie was aware of this. "I observed some chief executives at some Trusts doing that in a very technical way. It's not difficult really to write a strategy; it's whether that resonates and has any meaning with anybody other than the senior leadership team and the board which is really, really important. [If it doesn't] I mean, it will just fail." This is where the 'wings' of the airplane come in. In order to ensure that that the strategy flies, it is necessary to have everyone lifting it and propelling it forward. And that, as she stresses is the real leadership challenge, that requires alignment and purpose to be held with clarity across the organization.

"[The strategy] is likely to be set in the wrong direction without that broader engagement. For me, the purpose is a deeper sense of reason and direction. And it's that collective sense of connectivity and understanding—why we're here and what we're here to do—that is so important. And that is why the two wings of the jet are so critical because you can't get enough height, you can't get enough amplification in a Trust like mine without that."

So how does someone manage such an organization, keeping the strategy and objectives at the fore, while also ensuring that the culture and values are continually attended to and fostered? Pre-pandemic in 2019 Dame Jackie set out her core approach around this, in a five-page document called #FlourishAtWork Framework (read it here: **tinyurl.com/d4vua5kt**). It centres around three dimensions: Leadership; Strategy and Governance; and Networks of Activity. As she writes in the document of the third dimension: "This structure is dynamic, initiatives and sub initiatives coalesce and disband as needed.... this type of network activity typically morphs all the time and with ease. Since it contains no bureaucratic layers or command and control prohibitions, the network permits a level of individualism, creativity and innovation." It is easy to see how this approach enables the growth of purpose, as it creates the space and conditions for all employees to have some agency to build on the areas they see as most important to them, within the overall strategic framework.

This more fluid approach to culture and values also allows things to surface that would not do so in a more strictly controlled process. "I think that's where the central operating framework is so important, because things come into view. I operate on a 12-week cycle within the year. So of course, you've got your strategy, and then what we typically do in health, as most organizations do, is set your annual objectives so that you can try and break this down into bite-sized chunks that are meaningful for ward staff nurses or your head porter. And that's really tricky because you've got to disaggregate it at every level and create meaning at every level. And of course, stuff happens...."

It's not difficult to write a strategy; it's whether that has any meaning with anybody other than the senior leadership team which is really, really important.

At the time of speaking, UK nurses had just voted, for the first time in five decades, to go on strike, which definitely falls into the 'stuff happens' category. In such a high risk and purpose-led environment it is important to note that the strike is not just about pay, but also the low number of nurses employed, so that they are over-worked and fear for patient safety.

The prism through which Dame Jackie views this is wider than just the immediate boundaries of her organization. She sees that as her experience has grown, her understanding of the eco-system in which the Trust works has broadened too. "As you get more and more experienced in your job, you build a deeper sense of purpose in the broader sphere. I am very, very onnected with the health and wealth of the Northeast, as a region. And I do a lot of work to focus on driving up economic development and creating jobs." Specifically, she sees that social deprivation in the areas that the Trust serves, inevitably stokes the flow of poor health outcomes which then come into the hospitals. "I see part of my role as a big employer chief exec is about creating opportunities. People who wouldn't other-wise get it in those pockets of deprivation and inequality in our community. So, it's broader than just running the Trust. It's a broader sense of responsibility about the economic ecosystem." While the particular issue of the strikes will require a careful balancing act of understanding and appreciating the nurses' issues, she still needs to keep the service running. This plays to what she sees as a major role for the CEO of being the voice of the organization both internally and externally. Externally is simpler to understand, but the real energy is in the internal communications. Dame Jackie uses a lot of different channels to keep not just messages flowing through the Trust, but reinforcing and re-invigorating initiatives and essential values, to ensure that core purpose is kept alive and vibrant. These occur as blogs, social media, visits and being seen. "I think my job is to curate and narrate what's happening and try and make sense of it at the moment. It's how you how you make sense of empathizing with the cause."

Two Systems – One Culture

Dame Jackie keeps returning to the two distinct levels of leadership she provides, which are encapsulated in her Flourish framework. This is the two-system approach, one technical and highly structured, the other much less definable, but probably more impactful, that supports the 'human magic' element that people with purpose bring to organizations in their collective momentum, energy and drive.

The formal leadership work around managing the governance and strategic objectives, takes place at the top of the organization and is System 1. Dame Jackie notes "I am doing formal business hierarchically, some of the bureaucratic, but important governance stuff, with a very small minority of my staff", this is necessary and works, but then leaves a disconnect with the rest of the organization. This potential divide is crossed with her System 2 approach of Networks of Activity. This work amplifies and provides reach of the core objectives but allows everyone in the organization from ward secretaries and ancillary staff onwards to take initiative and play their parts.

As you get more and more experienced in your job, you build a deeper sense of purpose in the broader sphere. I am very, very connected with the health and wealth of the Northeast, as a region

Dame Jackie admits that the informality and looseness of System 2 would have concerned her when she was starting out as a CEO. But she has seen that by giving people the space and agency to initiate projects around things they are passionate about, is entirely positive. "Some of this stuff in System 2 you can't control, it's just happening. And it's like a thousand flowers blooming." She goes on to point out that people will do the things they are passionate about to an extent anyway, so it is better to create a supportive space for it.

The NHS is a force for good, but its impact on climate, for instance, is large, whether from the high heating costs, waste output or use of toxic substances; people in the organization at all levels are passionate about healthcare and many also passionate about climate change, so allowing room for them to take initiatives and push forward projects that alleviate some of the impact leverages energy and purpose that is already in the organization. "People want to talk about the climate emergency; and people want to understand how in health, we play our part. And so, they'll go at it, whether I'm overseeing it or caring about it or not."

It is important to understand that the model only works because of both systems though. System 2 can only operate if System 1 is in place. Healthcare is a high-risk sector and appalling outcomes can develop if the governance and risk management is not in place. However, she is clear that if you only have System 1 in place, then the operating culture can turn negative quickly too. "The risk management keeps us safe; it alerts us to the potential for harm, ... the formal mechanism highlights or triggers a flag and so it's so important. But actually, if used badly, it creates an environment of fear, of defence, rather than of curiosity."

Enabling and developing the culture and mindsets to achieve this environment is neither quick nor simple, and her NHS Trust is focused on strengthening and evolving those capacities. "We are investing a lot in the leadership development of our top 250 leaders around mindset and behaviour; and how you create the environment where people can flourish and not feel inhibited and not feel fearful. And that takes a lot of work. It is part of the science as well as the art."

For Dame Jackie herself, she is aware that she has to attend to her own mindset and thinking on a regular basis too. She acknowledges that she is a conceptual thinker and an introvert, so her first responses to problems and emerging issues is to mindmap and reflect to make greater sense of them, before she actively brings in close colleagues to share issues with, to get that broader perspective and reflection. In addition, she has regular coaching, something she has engaged with for many years, and seeks out peers in other sectors beyond the NHS to get input, alternative views and to be challenged on her thinking.

"Some of this stuff in System 2 you can't control, it's just happening. And it's like a thousand flowers blooming."

The NHS is a massive, complex institution. The whole nation is hugely vested in it, both as patients or relatives of patients and as seeing it as a reflection of who we are. Ultimately it is guided by the current political administration–and as such becomes a punchbag for opposition politicians to attack the government. Beyond all that, it is an institution that needs to work well for everyone's health and well-being, one that employs many devoted and purposeful people passionate about making it do that.

Dame Jackie Daniel long ago mastered the technical side, but sees the difference in outcomes now, as she did when she started out as a nurse, as resting heavily on how healthy the culture within the organization is and how it is nurtured and strengthened. That is a job that can never be completed, it needs constant attention and effort – and experience. All of which she brings with clear purpose.

Roland Deiser in conversation
with Harvard Business School
professor Ranjay Gulati

Deep Purpose

Roland Deiser

Ranjay – your most recent book is called *Deep Purpose*.
What made you write about that topic, given your original
background on growth strategy, alliances and M&A?

Ranjay Gulati

If you would have told me five years ago, I'm going to
write a book about purpose, I would have said, you're
crazy, no way. I was somebody who studied unlock-
ing growth in businesses in good times and bad. I
started out with a focus on organic growth, then
moving on to growth through joint ventures, partnerships, and acquisitions – strategy work. I soon
realized that strategy alone doesn't cut it – to succeed
you need to focus on implementation. Strategic doing
and mobilization of people became important. I found
out that for some companies mission and purpose is not
just a generic wallpaper statement but something much
bigger than that. They use it to unlock the organization,
unlock the growth potential of companies. Until then I hadn't
thought much about purpose.

Also, working with start-ups and founders I discovered that their purpose meant intentionality – the ambition to change the world. There was something missing in my own understanding of growth, in what it takes to achieve your fullest potential. It was something fundamental – also on a very personal level, myself included: if we want to live to our fullest potential as human beings we must know our purpose.

RD That's a big step – from looking at growth and strategic dynamics to focusing on purpose. What is it, in essence, that fascinates you most?

RG Let's think about what the word purpose really means. It is not a new word. It's been around forever. The ancient Greeks talked about purpose. The ancient Indians talked about purpose, the Chinese talked about purpose, every ancient civilization talked about purpose. And every religion talks about purpose – on the individual level. The application of purpose to organization is a relatively new idea.

The Stanford psychologist William Denning defines purpose as a stable and generalized intention to accomplish something that is meaningful to the self AND consequential for the world beyond the self. So if we bring intentionality into our life, we become more purposeful, we become more focused, we know how to make choices and trade-offs. Now, if individuals benefit from having a purpose that propels me, motivates me, and energizes me, can we think about this construct for an organization?

Unfortunately the notion of organizational purpose has been hijacked in the business lexicon by the left and the right. People say "Oh, purpose is all non-profit stuff." Or purpose is all shareholder value only. This is a meaningless debate.

I soon realized that strategy alone doesn't cut it – to succeed you need to focus on implementation.

Ranjay Gulati

Because every business should have intention. When you think long-term about your business, you have to think about your employees. You have to think about your customers, you have to think about the communities where you operate. You have to think about the shareholders. And you have to possibly think about the planet too. All of this matters.

If we want to live to our fullest potential as human beings we must know our purpose.

RD So, there is a social architecture behind purpose? Because if purpose impacts the world, it must reach beyond just the system that has the purpose but also the systems that are impacted by this purpose. This interplay may shape the overall development of purpose.

RG That's a great question. When I started my research for the book, I found so many companies practice what I call superficial purpose. They think of it as a PR exercise – everybody has one, so we need to have one. And guess what – it doesn't do anything, it's meaningless. The other thing I realized was that purpose is not just in the purpose statement. If you read Microsoft's purpose that Satya Nadella and his team came up with, it says to empower every person and every organization on the planet to achieve more. That seems very flat, generic, copy and paste. But what I learned from them was that it wasn't the statement; it's the nine months they spent debating what it is, and the meaning it gives to them. To the outside, it may look like empty words, full of platitudes, and cliches. But for them, there's a lot of meaning in these words when they are making decisions about resource allocation, or budgeting, or R&D, or hiring.

That's why I called the book *Deep Purpose*, because it's not just about purpose statements. It's about what are the problems you want to profitably solve for the world. What value do you want to create? How do you want to create it, and for whom? I exist to create value to benefit our customers, our shareholders, our employees, our communities, and the planet. Every business exists to solve a problem.

RD Well – GE, for example, has a great purpose statement prominently on their home page: "We rise to the challenge of

The ancient Greeks talked about purpose. The ancient Indians talked about purpose. The Chinese talked about purpose. Every ancient civilization talked about purpose.

building a world that works". Still, they have been in disarray and are still struggling to regain at least some of their past glory.

RG I guess you're asking if purpose is a necessary and sufficient condition to succeed – and the answer is no. Purpose is one of the levers available. You still need a strategy; you still need an organization to implement the strategy. You can't live on purpose alone. In fact, it gives purpose a bad rep when CEOs who are not performing try to hide behind their purpose and say 'we're trying to follow our purpose – it takes some time.' This happened actually in a tragic way at Danone. Emmanuel Faber, an amazing leader, deeply committed to transform the mission of Danone as a food company. But he couldn't deliver results. And at some point investors lost patience with him. Purpose includes shareholders – they give you the license to do all these other things. You can't not deliver for them. The idea that I'm a long-term company, I don't deliver short-term – that does not work.

You also asked me where does purpose come from? Now, if you're a start-up company, you may create a purpose that is usually an extension of the founders' own beliefs. The founders of Johnson & Johnson wrote the credo that persists even today. Such organizations have a shadow of the past that lingers on. They may have changed it many times, but it's still there. Some-

times the purpose seems to be lost and you have to detect it through retrospective sense-making. The challenge is not to get hijacked by the past. The idea is to get inspired by the past and leverage this inspiration to shape your future.

RD I read your recent piece in HBR on that . I think the question is, can you even escape your DNA? I strongly believe there is something like an organizational DNA, which comes very much from the founders, usually. Then it develops over time, founders die, new generations come in. But you still cannot totally escape your identity. Which leads me to the relationship between purpose and identity. How do they relate?

RG Purpose and identity are very connected constructs. Identity is really about how do I see myself. It's a construct of how do I present myself to the world. So it can be social identity, which is, how do I see myself in relation to the world? How do I perceive myself, and how do I want to be perceived by others. That's identity. Purpose, on the other hand answers the question 'Why do I exist?'

RD I guess both concepts are very relevant in the context of large organizations or business ecosystems, where the role of purpose is also to mitigate the centrifugal forces that come with empowering the periphery so it can better engage with the external partner universe. Here purpose is one thing that keeps systems together. How do you see that?

RG It's fascinating to apply the concept of purpose to ecosystems. A lot of ecosystems are built around one or two or three companies that create a larger ecosystem around them, and it's imperative that they share a common purpose. There are classic failures in this context. For example Nokia – they tried to build a whole ecosystem around a software platform that would compete against Microsoft, Apple and others. But it was not driven by a shared purpose; it was really Nokia, pushing their agenda on everybody – and nobody bought in. Creating a purpose together creates a shared objective. It creates clarity in terms of roles and expectations. Crafting a shared purpose for an ecosystem could be a wonderful exercise to build alignment and shared understanding.

RD It's really a twofold challenge, I think. To succeed in the complex dynamics of an ecosystem, a company must know who they are and why they are doing this. If they don't, they are

Crafting a shared purpose for an ecosystem could be a wonderful exercise to build alignment and shared understanding

easily replaceable and may get torn apart by strong partners. So, first is your own purpose. But then you need also a purpose for the ecosystem, which can be a delicate process among partners there are no a priori governance mechanisms they can fall back on. I don't know how you see this.

RG I think you're right. And there's a reason why more than 50% of partnerships fail. And nobody knows how many ecosystems fail – probably more. A huge issue among many is goal alignment. The lack of clarity of individual goals as well as shared goals. It's easy to write something down that serves as purpose, but how do you operationalize it? Some companies that I've seen will turn purpose into a set of guiding principles, actionable principles that are rules translated from their purpose. Others will try to create KPIs from it. EY (Ernst & Young, a major global accounting firm), measures every partner on social value, customer value, employee value, and enterprise value. Their KPIs are tied to these four dimensions, which are directly a result of their purpose. It is a challenge to operationalize purpose, and then cascade it into the core. And I think this is a huge challenge for many organizations that talk about purpose, but they don't really know how to make it happen. This has been the bulk of my book, this purpose to action problem, what is also called the knowing-doing gap? And it gets worse. The further down the organization, the understanding of purpose exponentially decays.

Social identity is 'how do I see myself in relation to the world?' Purpose on the other hand answers the question 'Why do I exist?'

RD But there is also purpose on lower levels of a system. People come in with a certain purpose into an organization, a department has a certain purpose. I guess translating this into an organizational purpose, or even an ecosystem purpose is not trivial. There's always a structural conflict between the various system levels of purpose that are there. If they align, great. If they don't align, people leave, and ecosystems fall apart.

RG Let's go back in time and say you and I were talking to the leaders of Nokia, Ericsson, Samsung, and a few others who were trying to build a shared platform. And their idea was that smartphones are going to take off, they're going to create massive opportunity. We each have our own phones, but if we have a common platform we can do our own hardware on top of that platform. But we build a robust operating system that will be open source. And by doing so we create massive opportunities in the world where everybody, from farmers in poor countries to CEOs – can access their device and have a powerful way to improve, enhance and enrich their lives. Let's do that. Would the outcome have been different? If they had thought about that, if they had created a shared understanding where all of us are going to benefit? But they didn't do it. Google did it with Android. Or the auto industry. What if they would have come together around battery technology – they wouldn't be dealing with Tesla having 65% of market share of the electric car business. They were unable to imagine collective action. Purpose maybe is a way to enhance collective action through ecosystems and platforms and partnerships, by creating a shared understanding. It's a very interesting idea that I think hasn't been pursued enough.

RD Interesting you mention the automotive industry. There were actually efforts to team up between BMW and Daimler to create a car share service and other innovative solutions that they together would host, but it totally fell apart. And it's not only the lack of willingness – if you have incumbent companies like Nokia and Ericson, or Daimler and BMW, coming together with good intentions but a legacy mindset, chances are they still will be disrupted by somebody fresh who comes in with a different logic – often from outside the industry. Like Google did with Android, like Musk did with Tesla.

When you think about your purpose, it forces you to think about the value proposition you're creating, and for whom, and whether it is relevant or not today

RG This is a really interesting conversation. My colleague and friend Rebecca Henderson, who studies innovation, postulates that having a purpose can actually make you more innovative. I expand on that in my own book. When you think about your purpose, it forces you to think about the value proposition you're creating, and for whom, and whether it is relevant or not today. Because you are not so focused on products or services, you're focused on the problem space you want to operate in. So, you say I'm a mobility company, I'm not a combustion engine company. I'm a communication company, I'm not a device company. If you do that thought experiment first, it allows you to potentially constantly be questioning whether you have the right solutions to address problems. Thinking in terms of problem space creates the possibility to think beyond. Sadly, incumbent companies are generally horrible at innovation, and they kill themselves. Netflix did not kill Blockbuster. Blockbuster killed Blockbuster. BlackBerry killed Blackberry, Sears killed Sears, Motorola killed Motorola. Polaroid killed Polaroid. Kodak killed Kodak. Why couldn't Kodak do what Fuji did? Both of them had 50% market share of the film industry globally.

RD Yes, the famous disease of the leader.

RG I don't have a definitive answer on this, but my hypothesis is if Kodak would have been thinking about purpose more broadly, like 'we are an imaging company, we use images to enable the world to operate in a better way", perhaps they might have not been so much fixated on film. I'm just speculating here with you. I don't have the data.

RD I think the DNA of successful companies is very difficult to escape from. It's very hard for Daimler to deal with the fact that in the enlarged mobility space, their hardware may not be the dominant thing anymore. How do you re-shape mindsets – and the related operating models, supply chain architectures, deployed assets, and more? The Mercedes Museum in Stuttgart is a powerful symbol for this conundrum: here you can admire the first combustion engine, the first car, invented by Daimler. Mr. Daimler himself drove that car – actually, during PR events Daimler CEOs once in a while get into this car. This is the myth, the story, the identity – the purpose really – of Daimler. How can you transcend this DNA to innovate beyond?

RG Well, once in a while you have to revisit, refresh your purpose. The beauty of the Fuji story is that Fuji said, 'We are not a film company. We are much bigger than that. We're a diagnostic imaging company. So, how do we reimagine ourselves as an imaging company?' They also said, we're a chemical company, we understand chemicals. So how can we leverage our chemical expertise? Companies periodically have to do that and refresh. Another great example is Microsoft, which developed its purpose from Bill Gates credo 'a computer on every desk and in every home' to Satya Nadella's mission to 'empower every person and organization on the path to achieve more.' And you can see it builds on the previous purpose statement.

> *If Kodak had thought about purpose more broadly, like 'we are an imaging company, we use images to enable the world to operate in a better way', perhaps they might have not been so fixated on film.*

RD Leveraging the tension between the past and the future is a really powerful way to look at it – I like it. One last thing I am curious about: Your journey brought you from thinking about growth strategies to a very successful book on *Deep Purpose*. What is next for Ranjay Gulati? Is there a next book?

RG Yes, there is already a next book in the works. I think it'll be an extension of my work on purpose, looking at the role of leadership and leaders in our world. For the last 10 years, I've been collecting stories of leaders who accomplished extraordinary things. What did it take to achieve what they did? What motivated them and inspired them to move that direction? So that's my next project – an extension of what I've been doing on Purpose.

RD That's interesting – you continue to move from the hard facts to the softer facts.

RG Maybe as I'm getting older I have been drawn to the more ambiguous side of business. Because I think that's where a lot of the value addition happens – and that's where we have the least understanding. I'm an engineer by training, so I try to bring an engineering sensibility to softer things. That's what I'm trying to do.

Ranjay Gulati is the Paul R. Lawrence MBA Class of 1942 Professor of Business Administration at Harvard Business School. He is the author of Deep Purpose: The Heart and Soul of High-Performance Companies. (Harper Business, 2022). You will find a review of his book on page 202.

Roland Deiser is Chairman of the Center for the Future of Organization at the Drucker School of Management and Co-publisher of Developing Leaders Quarterly.

Ralf Schneider

Purpose and Performance: The next generation

With the arrival of Next-Gen organizations, we witness the rise of the human-centric enterprise and the dominance of intangible over tangible assets. Intellectual capital, human capital and social capital are moving to the centre of the performance equation.

The source of strategic competitive advantage has shifted from "what, we produce", to "how, efficiently we are doing it", to "why, we do, what we do". In other words, the source of strategic competitive advantage has moved from product, to process to purpose (Schneider 1998). Of course, all elements are still very important, "What" and "How" we produce remain key table stakes of competitiveness. However, differentiation comes from the ability to attract talent, create share of heart with customers and build trust-based relationships across and beyond the organization to allow for inclusion, innovation and learning from the future.

The Changing Source of Strategic Competitive Advantage

Ralf Schneider, Better Business (1999)

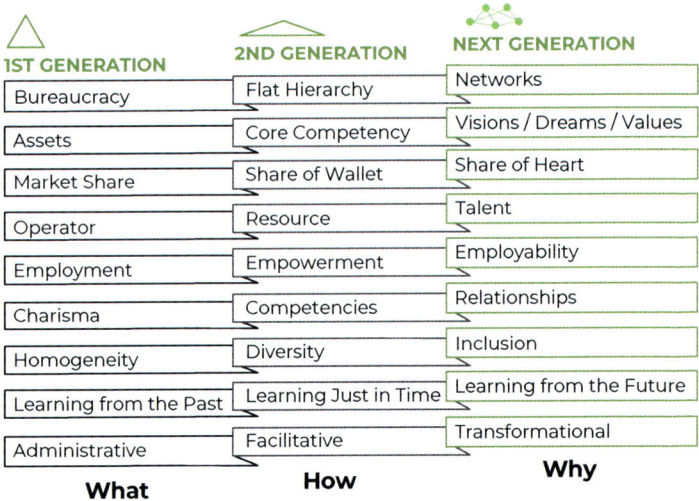

1ST GENERATION	2ND GENERATION	NEXT GENERATION
Bureaucracy	Flat Hierarchy	Networks
Assets	Core Competency	Visions / Dreams / Values
Market Share	Share of Wallet	Share of Heart
Operator	Resource	Talent
Employment	Empowerment	Employability
Charisma	Competencies	Relationships
Homogeneity	Diversity	Inclusion
Learning from the Past	Learning Just in Time	Learning from the Future
Administrative	Facilitative	Transformational
What	**How**	**Why**

In Next-Gen business, where semi-autonomous units, ad-hoc working groups, agile structures, networks, and eco-systems become the vehicles by which companies deliver their work, purpose becomes a source of cohesion, reduced transaction cost and elevated performance. Employer brands that capture share of heart energise the commitment, engagement, and motivation of talent.

The source of strategic competitive advantage has shifted from "what we produce" to "how efficiently we are doing it" to "why we do what we do". In other words, it has moved from product to process to purpose.

Purpose gives performance meaning, beyond the transaction. It turns "Human Doings" into "Human Beings". It activates a deeper level of contract. With the right fit, the organization can become an extension and expression of who I am, why I exist and what I am here for. In fact, for some, "Work" itself can become the purpose (or at least the conduit through which I express it). We witness this in the entrepreneurial start-up space of the digital economy, where individual purpose and organizational purpose are aligned (or have huge overlap). This typically has a positive impact on performance. (Do what I love, and love what I do; 90 hours and loving it.)

Purpose thus can become a social marker and part of the personal brand through an implicit moral contract that exists between organization and individual talent.

This can of course create potential pathologies. Pathologies of purpose need to be managed carefully and responsibly or can lead to cult-like compliance, self-exploitation and burn out, exclusion of outsiders, cause-based myopia leading to a lack of connection with reality in pursuit of a cause, or even fraud to "cover up" what was done in pursuit of the purpose,

Purpose gives performance meaning, beyond the transaction. It turns "Human Doings" into "Human Beings".

without the right moral compass in place. A recent example would be the FTX cryptocurrency exchange led by Sam Bankman-Fried who had been a voluble proponent of 'effective altruism', until his business collapsed, and is now indicted on fraud in his attempts to sustain it.

Future ready organizations need to get three contracts right

In the internal perspective, purpose does not exist in isolation. It is part of an interconnected set of contracts between the individual and the organization. These contracts need to be in sync in the perception of individual talent to be effective.

At the base sits the **legal or commercial contract**. 'I am here because I am paid for it' ("What"/First Generation). This contract defines the formal incentives in return for the employees' contribution.

This needs to be complemented by a **psychological contract**. 'I am here because I like it here'. (How/2nd Generation). This contract is more implicit and depends on how you feel about the culture fit and the way you are being treated by the organization and by colleagues.

The Third level is the **moral contract**. 'I am here because I belong here'. This contract is rooted in a deeply understood and shared purpose or a "cause" ("Why"/, 3rd generation). It expresses why the employee is here. The moral contract is usually operationalized through values or principles linking it to standards of business ethics and the psychological contract.

I would argue, that while not all organizations need to have an "integrator" value proposition (where responsible leadership sits at its core and all stakeholders are considered in its decisions to serve the greater good by doing the right thing) and a cause-based purpose, we will see more companies choosing that position in the future. Because they aim to be more effective in creating sustainable competitive advantage in a next generation environment.

The Three Levels of Contact Between The Organisation And The Individual

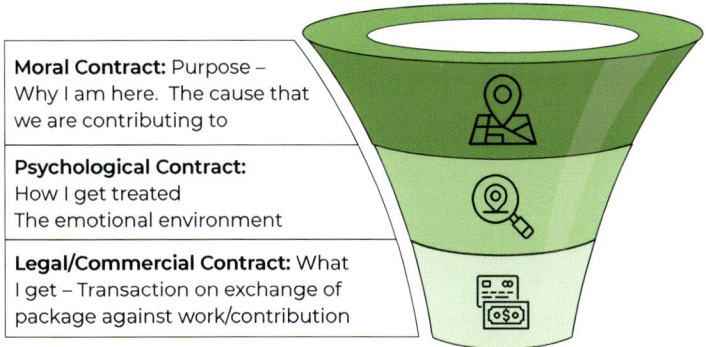

Moral Contract: Purpose – Why I am here. The cause that we are contributing to

Psychological Contract: How I get treated The emotional environment

Legal/Commercial Contract: What I get – Transaction on exchange of package against work/contribution

In Next-Gen environments all three levels of internal contract need to be in place.

Leaders must ask themselves, what business they want to create. All things being equal, purpose often becomes the differentiator, specifically for talent with choice. The quest for purpose becomes a choice of the right position on the purpose curve and the right fit with the individual purpose of talent.

For talent, the moral contract often is a part of the expression of their overall personal brand and identity. It is an expression of their choice of who they want to be associated with. It is a manifestation of their intention, expressed through visible membership to a social group with a shared purpose. In this way, purpose creates a sense of belonging.

In Next-Gen businesses, the definition, alignment, and the authentic delivery of purpose is at the core of the leadership job. Purpose manifests itself in the decisions leaders take and the quality of trust-based relationships they build to keep systems effective. This is experienced through relationships that align with purpose and values.

Therefore, the quality of leadership is so important to next generation businesses. It also has become more demanding on leaders' personal mastery and maturity. This may be one of the reasons why CEOs and CHROs see an increasing gap of leadership in their businesses, despite increasing investment into leadership development. Purpose is not a "comms piece", it is the experience through aligned decisions and role modelling. Leading in this context is a constant quest of presence, awareness, authenticity, and integrity. Next-Gen leadership is demanding, complex and personal.

Structures and processes are the base skeleton, while purpose and values are the lifeblood that makes distributed/ semi-autonomous systems productive. It is leadership that creates the glue that makes network structures work. Next-Gen organizations do not just need diverse talent as elements of this network. They need the glue to bind them together through shared meaning and values. This is also the essence of meaningful inclusion. As leadership in networks is ultimately about building trust-based relationships, it is permanent work. There is no final state or stable equilibrium that, once achieved, can be taken for granted. Relationships are dynamic, diverse, (sometimes) disrupted and always personal.

In turn, this means that the development of purpose-driven leadership needs to become a key competence of Next-Gen organizations, both at individual and at organizational level.

What is the role of leadership development

Purpose and values are easy to declare, but hard to deliver in day-to-day decisions and actions. Therefore, the quest for purpose is also the quest for the right quality of leadership. At a strategic level it is senior leadership that sets the right purpose and ensures alignment with society. It is then the job of leaders at all levels to translate and transmit purpose. It activates meaning on a day-to-day basis in all actions and all relationships. Without leadership, purpose remains an intention or abstract claim.

This takes us to the question of how to develop purpose-based leadership.

Here it is useful to differentiate between organizational leadership development and individual leader development.

Organizational Leadership Development

This is the process of defining and delivering the right leadership strategy in alignment with purpose, values, and strategy of the organization. It sets the expectations for leadership in any given business. This typically includes the following aligned elements of a leadership strategy.

In some cases, the organizational leadership development includes the process of facilitating the (re-)definition of purpose, values, and behaviours itself. Typically, this happens at exceptional moments in a company's lifecycle. Examples are crisis/restructuring, merger& acquisitions, launch of a new strategy, digital transformation.

Aligning Strategy and Leadership Brand

Leadership Context

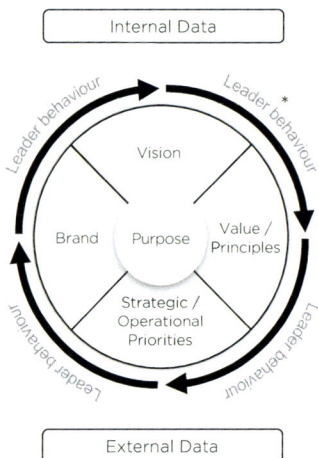

| Internal Data |

Vision

Brand Purpose Value / Principles

Strategic / Operational Priorities

Leader behaviour

| External Data |

Leadership Brand Definition

Leadership Core

| 1 Strategist |
| 2 Executor |
| 3 Talent Manager |
| 4 Capability Builder |
| 5 Personal Mastery |

Leadership Differentiators

| 1 |
| 2 |
| 3 |

Purpose manifests itself in the decisions leaders take and the quality of trust-based relationships they build to keep systems effective.

Leadership Strategy

```
!  Objectives
!  Employee Value Proposition
!  Attraction / Selection
!  Recruitment
!  Deployment
!  Learning
!  Talent Mgt. / Succession
!  Perf. Mgt
!  Reward
!  Diversity
!  Engagement
```

Leadership Metrics

*Based on Collective Ambition Compass, Doug Ready and Leadership Brand, Dave Ulrich

The role of Organizational Leadership Development is predominantly culture development and alignment, starting with purpose.

At an organizational level it starts with system alignment and organizational alignment to close a potential purpose and culture gap. At the individual level it often requires a mindset shift to align behaviours

The work for leadership development can therefore be described as orchestrating the alignment at the following four levels.

Aligning Leadership and Culture with Purpose and Values

Layers of culture	Elements of alignment	Potential risk/gap
System Alignment	Organizational Purpose & Values with Stakeholders and Society	Purpose Gap
	Organizational Values with Strategy	Mindset Gap
Organisation Alignment	Current culture with desired culture	Current Culture Gap
Behavioural Alignment	Individual Values with Organization Values	Values Fit Gap
	Individual Values with Actual Behaviour	Individual Integrity Gap
	Actual Behaviour with Organization Values	Individual Integrity Gap
Process Alignment	Process and Systems with organisational Values	Organization Design Gap

A healthy culture is a product of careful alignment of all interdependent layers

At each level a lack of alignment creates a specific gap between promise and reality and can lead to reduced performance, risky decisions, or breakdown of relationships with internal or external stakeholders. Purpose and values are part of the moral contract. It is powerful when it is kept. If the gap is too big it can have a negative impact on people, clients, and results.

Identifying and closing these gaps is a key role for organizational leadership development. Ideally, this alignment is based on data, identifying the current gaps at each level. This can be achieved through the combination of several analytic tools and methodologies.

This multi-level alignment will require a dynamic process of organizational learning and experimentation which in turn offers a big opportunity to the leadership development function to re-define its role and relevance in contributing to organizational performance. It also opens the window for innovation regarding tools, competencies, and formats of organizational leadership development.

This starts with a better understanding of the changing role of leadership in next generation environments and organizations. In fluid structures and networks, the role of the individual leader changes. In our work with clients, we suggest defining their current and future profile relative to the 10 roles of leadership in Next-Gen organizations.

All roles are closely tied to purpose. However, specifically the roles of:
- Ambassador
- Anchor
- Host
- Accelerator
- Gardener

show how leaders can practically help to build a purpose-led business.

10 Characteristics of Next Generation Leaders

Ambassador

Champions, represents and communicates the purpose, vision, actions and capabilities of the system to all its stakeholders, engages to negotiate ways of working and open interaction, resolves conflict, predominantly with internal and external clients.

Protector

Protects the people, budget, processes and objectives of the system and its freedom to operate to achieve its purpose. This includes the provision of the right resources to sustain the system through its lifecycle.

Explorer

Actively seeks out new and unknown territory, creates new maps and finds a new course of action. Challenges the current status and paradigm, easily and actively travels across boundaries of disciplines, technologies and other domains, while letting go of the "known".

Anchor

Role-models, enforces, evolves norms, values and rituals of the system. A key element of this role is to anchor and root the integrity of the system and its purpose.

Architect

Designs and re-designs relevant processes, policies, physical environment and technology in a way that they are supportive and fit for innovation and co-creation.

Translator

Designs and re-designs relevant processes, policies, physical environment and technology in a way that they are supportive and fit for innovation and co-creation.

Host

Invites and welcomes new people and ideas. Creates and holds open spaces for emergence and evolution of ideas and relationships between people, ideas and things.

Accelerator

Removes roadblocks, trailblazes andcreates a fast track for promising ideas in service of the overarching objective and in accordance with purpose and values of the system.

Integrator

Integrates new people, ideas, processes and capabilities to crystalise and scale solutions across existing and new (non-traditional elements of a networkdynamic /ecosystem.

Gardener

Nurtures and develops people, identifies, selects and deselects talent and places them for fit and growth with care for their long-term wellbeing and optimal contribution to the whole.

Next-Gen organizations do not just need diverse talent as elements of this network. They need the glue to bind them together through shared meaning and values.

Having worked with hundreds of leaders around the world we learnt that to deploy these roles effectively leaders need to acquire new skillsets. But more importantly, these roles require the individual and collective development of new mindsets. These mindsets are closely connected with understanding individual and organizational purpose, values and their manifestation in leadership behaviour. These mindsets express a higher level of awareness and consciousness required of leaders in purpose-led organizations.

Working with many diverse organizations around the world, we have identified six mindsets (outlined opposite and overleaf) to be essential and universal for effective Next-Gen leaders.

The development of these mindsets requires a process of self-discovery. This leads us to the hallmarks of effective individual leader development for next generation businesses.

The Six Mindsets of Next Generation Leadership
Ralf Schneider, Better Business (2021)

Courage

- Is comfortable to let go of control and allow an open outcome
- Understands and overcomes fear (where necessary or important)
- Is comfortable with operating outside own comfort zone
- Is able to hold an open space for self and others for experimentation, evolution and emergence as a social process
- Operates from a place of purpose
- Is conscious in taking smart risk
- Is able and willing to seek deep self-reflection in pursuit of purpose, meaning and fulfilment

Humility

- Puts oneself in service of others and the wider purpose of he system
- Doesn't seek the lime- light, but enables others and celebrates their achievements
- Leads by supporting from behind
- Takes satisfaction from creating space for others to progress, grow and contribute
- Can let go of "Ego", position and self-centredness
- Is aware of the limits of own knowledge, wisdom and truth

Cont/..

The Six Mindsets of Next Generation (...cont)

Curiosity

- Consciously and continuously scans the wider context and current situation for opportunities to learn
- Observes with an open mind
- Suspends judgement
- Actively tries to identify blind spots
- Seeks and embraces feedback
- Engages with intense presence
- Appreciates and values new and different ideas and perspectives
- Asks open questions
- Is inquisitive and interested in a wide range of topics, people and views

Compassion

- Easily connects with people at an emotional/human level
- Is aware of bias and can suspend cynicism
- Comfortable with self-disclosure and vulnerability
- Can walk in other's shoes and empathise
- Enjoys diversity and can build bridges to inclusion with open heart
- Instills trust in self and others
- Builds trust-based relationships
- Engages with others in open and honest dialogue
- Listens with empathy
- Cares about others' wellbeing

Integrity

- Aligns their thoughts, words and actions
- Is true to and stands up for their values
- Speaks truth to power
- Delivers on their promises
- Willingly takes responsibility and accountability and encourages other to do the same

Optimism

- Is realistic and positive in outlook on life and own capabilities
- Enters relationships with trust and positivity
- Can see a brighter future in adversity
- Can forgive self and others and move forward
- Can see an opportunity for learning in every problem or conflict
- Sees life and work as a stream of own choices
- Takes action with appropriate confidence and energy

Individual Leader Development

At the individual level, the quest for purpose is the alignment or (better) fit, between individual and organizational purpose. For leaders it is the result of a deep dive into their own purpose. It also is a deep dive into understanding their own internal alignment (Integrity) and the congruence between their leadership intention versus their actual impact on others.

Next-Gen organizations understand that leadership excellence starts with individual self-discovery. This self-discovery is not self-serving. It sits within a compass of relevant stakeholder relationships, within which individual leaders operate and need to become more effective. Leader development therefore starts with understanding individual purpose and identity in context of organizational purpose.

The Better Business Leadership Compass

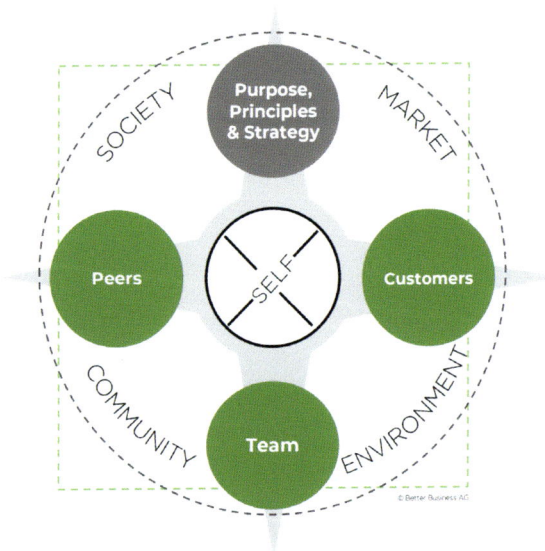

© Better Business AG

Purpose and values cannot be taught. They need to be discovered and embodied through experience and exploration, linked to personal and organizational context.

In this context, the personal quest for purpose is more than mindfulness training in pursuit of personal happiness, enlightenment and fulfilment. It requires a thoughtfully designed journey of discovery that allows leaders to understand who they are, how their purpose and values fit with their organization and what their own level of integrity is in delivering their purpose and values in their leadership (with clients/peers and their teams). They also need to understand their own leadership footprint (impact and contribution) in bringing purpose and values alive in their business relationships.

Over the past years, many leadership programs have picked this up and added mindfulness, purpose, well-being, resilience etc. to the list of topics and methodologies for individual development programs. However, often these programs fall short of making the connection to the business and development of shared purpose as a source of commitment, energy, and sense of belonging. Worse, when the course is over, they might spark deeper scepticism as to what the organization's real intention and purpose is, when faced with current organizational culture and its reality back at work. Lack of alignment creates a lack of trust and integrity. It ultimately disenfranchises leaders. To avoid this, organizational leadership development and individual leader development need to be in sync.

Next generation leadership development is not about teaching content. Purpose and values cannot be taught. They need to be discovered and embodied through experience and exploration, linked to personal and organizational context.

There are many ways in which this can be orchestrated. What we found works best, are carefully designed learning journeys built on exploration, dialogue, and co-creation, built around a personal quest for purpose.

Whether at organizational and/or individual level, it should be carefully thought through and designed from a holistic perspective to be effective and deliver the desired impact.

Conclusion

The push for more accountability and the need to meet future stakeholder expectations will raise the bar for business on purpose and conduct and require a broader definition of value.

Next gen business strategies and structures will require authentic, purpose-driven alignment at five levels to build future ready organizations and cultures.

Leadership is the key driver and enabler of this process and therefore needs to be ready to shift its role and mindset to enable sustainable and inclusive businesses.

Future focused leadership development has a double role in this. It needs to understand and embrace the new role and responsibilities of leaders and find new forms for organizational and individual learning, to close the gaps and focus on building trust-based relationships across stakeholder groups, rooted in an authentic purpose.

Ralf Schneider *is Managing Partner of www.betterbusinesspartners. biz and Chairman of Digital Circles AG.*

Also read Ralf Schneider's additional piece on the DLQ website, which explores the broader context of our Quest for Purpose. **developingleadersquarterly.com/ dlq40-purpose-performance-prologue-ralf-schneider/**

Sertac Yeltekin

How to Embark on a New Purposeful Journey

n the summer of 2017, after 25 years in the corporate world, I embarked on a new personal and professional journey that helped me discover a purposeful job, a new continent – Asia, an entrepreneurial spirit concealed in me that I was not previously aware of, and a new way of working that came to be known as the future of work, where remotely connected professionals sharing a vision and mission collaborate. That is a lot to tell so I will unpack the main steps in this journey, shed some light on my key challenges and dilemmas, and reveal the emotional story behind my passage from the corporate world to the entre- preneurship of impact investing.

I hope my story is helpful for those seeking to jump from the corporate world to a new work experience underscored by self-application, self-motivation, and alignment of purpose in an uncharted territory of new knowledge and previously unexplored geography.

Entrepreneurship, let alone aligning purpose with profit, was less of a choice until later stages in one's life

How to Let Go and Unlearn

I had spent more than two decades of my working life in financial services and management consulting helping large companies – local, regional and global – create value for their shareholders in Europe. I had learned the art of navigating the organizational structures of large companies by building alliances with colleagues and creating the buy-in to help to push an agenda while managing the expectations of bosses, peers and collaborators. In return I relied on a paycheck, generous benefits and bonuses . I was the product of my generation that graduated in the 1980s and 90s when management consulting and finance were the main two alternatives to succeed in the work environment. Entrepreneurship, let alone aligning purpose with profit, was less of a choice until later stages in one's life. The world that I was accustomed to was that of corporations with their own rules and regulations mostly insulated from the dilemmas and challenges of early-stage companies.

In the summer of 2017, I got a call from an old friend from my consulting years to join an impact investing fund in Southeast Asia that she had founded – when I heard the proposal it was as if neurons in my brain were lit up. I felt a strong sense of excitement and energy, in order of relevance: the location of this new job – Southeast Asia, a region that I had never lived in; a job I had never done before – venture capital focused on impact investing; and a sense of purpose that came along with the job. The fund invested in early-stage companies that offered services and products to underserved populations, mostly at the bottom of the social pyramid with very limited access to affordable healthcare, education, energy, essential goods & services and financial services. I also felt a sense of fear, again, in order of relevance: letting go of the habits of the working life in large corporations, finding myself in a cultural environment different from that which I was used to in Europe and working with early-stage companies that did not necessarily need my skills.

What was impact investing, anyhow? Impact investing was coined as the new form investment to tackle the malaise of underdevelopment. The investment scheme that impact investing proposed was no longer through the transfer of funds and knowledge from international agencies such IMF, World Bank or IFC to governments of the developing world that had underpinned the world of development economics for the previous 60 years. Impact investment focused on sustaining and supporting private entrepreneurs who in turn tackle social and environmental issues by establishing enterprises that have a balanced view of impact and profit. The term was introduced by the Rockefeller Foundation in the aftermath of the 2008 financial crisis to deal with the excesses of capitalism that had focused on financial profits at the expense of society and environment. I had a somewhat vague notion of impact investing, I knew how to set up and manage mutual funds but possessed very limited knowledge in a closed-end venture fund. There was much to let go of from my previous world and unlearn many habits. I could no longer rely on a corporate structure – our fund was small, and its resources were limited. I could not stay within the comfort zone of my accustomed world of finance and orga-

There was much to let go of from my previous world and unlearn many habits. I could no longer rely on a corporate structure. I could not stay within the comfort zone

nizations, could no longer count on my knowledge of European organizational and work culture. I had to deal with fragile early-stage companies and its heroic founders who may or may not need the knowledge and skills that I had honed over the years.

How to Blend In

Balancing social and environmental impact with sustainable profits seemed like a reasonable thing to do but it has never been the impulse with which investment decisions were made in the past by private investors. It was a novel development to scrutinize and analyze the value of companies based on the purpose they had manifested in the social and environmental sphere and discover if they could also churn financial profits. In the past if a private individual or institution wanted to do good, it would set up a philanthropy arm and for investments they would seek companies doing what they did for centuries – churn out financial profits. There was nothing in between.

Impact investment tried to introduce a healthy dose of purpose to why people made investments: to ensure that our world remained on a course of sustainable growth so that neither long-term financial profits nor the world's delicate balance in society and environment are put at risk. If this was the sensible thing to do, why was it not on the map? First of all, social and environmental impact measurement techniques were either not developed or not sought for as criteria. Second, there was a net separation between society and environment on one end and profits on the other end. The two worlds never met. Social and environment justice that cut across intersectional lines – the North-South axis of economic development,

The two worlds never met. Social and environment justice that cut across intersectional lines – the North-South axis of economic development, gender, class, ethnicity – were never accounted for.

My moment of epiphany happened when a lawyer told me that he thought I was a tree-hugging hippie before I met him

gender, class, ethnicity – were never accounted for. Third, the social inequalities revealed by the 2008 financial crisis and the environmental mayhem with animals on the brink of extinction coupled with rising temperatures due to excessive extraction of the world's resources put the world as we know it at a risk not seen since the extinction of dinosaurs. Many new ways and initiatives were developed to bridge the gap between purpose and profit: the triple bottom line accounting of People, Planet, Profit, became a manifesto via conducting social and environmental accounting on par with financial accounting; the B-Corp movement certified companies on their adherence to "beneficial company status; the large international organizations such as the Global Impact Investing Network (GIIN) became the crossroads organization for the dialogue between the private and public sector as well as between the investor and the investee.

This new emerging world of impact investing was on the map even before the ESG investments were being increasingly adopted since 2018 by the finance mainstream as a solution to scale up impact. ESG, Environment, Social and Governance, is a blend of universal criteria that set the stage to assess whether a company is preventing harm in these three key areas while conducting its own business. Unlike ESG norms that stop at preventing harm, impact investment is instead focused on the intentionality of doing good. That intentionality of engaging in activities that generate good is at the core of impact investing and distinguishes it from the ESG movement.

When I started to work in the impact investing sector in 2017, these concepts were hardly known by the public or by mainstream finance. In a matter of five years, accelerated by the pandemic that revealed the fragility of the human experience, these concepts grew to become multi-trillion-dollar industries with dark and light sides that I will try to illustrate in the next sections. My moment of epiphany happened when a lawyer whose services in Singapore that I sought for an acquisition in Myanmar told me that he thought I was a tree-hugging hippie before I met him. The comment made me laugh and think at the same time. In the late 60s hippies were considered as dropouts from society and became the laughing-stock of the conservatives. A few years later they came to define an era.

How to navigate troubled waters: sustainability, its joys and discontents

By late 2018 I was quite settled in the world of impact investing, trying to understand what could be done better and differently. The light side of impact investment was that investors deployed capital to nascent entrepreneurial initiatives that tackled social and environmental issues through a for-profit enterprise – the quest for both impact and profit firmly anchored. This new breed of investors was patient, long-term oriented and largely unmoved by the whims of the market and expected a return on investment that balanced profits and purpose. Companies supported by these investors continued to create miracles despite insurmountable difficulties in South and Southeast Asia – to name a few, an Indian company that offers affordable cataract operations to the poor who otherwise would

Many impact investment projects were subscale, had thin margins and remained dependent on the support of impact investors throughout their life cycle. It was not sufficient to confine the term to the bottom of the pyramid

fall prey to loan sharks and remain indebted for generations; a Myanmar company that extends loans as little as $5 to the poor to build their own economic activities – against conventional wisdom, the customers of this company rarely default on their loans where the average delinquency rate was less that 1% of total customers; a coffeehouse chain present in Vietnam, Cambodia and Laos that employ victims of human trafficking; an off-grid energy company in India that offer affordable energy to the poor. Around the globe, impact investors were also active in extending trillion dollars of debt facilities to prop up affordable real estate, sustainable infrastructure, green energy, and accessible financial services to support financial inclusion.

While public or semi-public Development Finance Institutions (DFIs) such as sovereign funds from developed countries dedicated themselves to international development, progressive foundations and family offices from the West focused on investments with low financial return/high impact. Asian investors were predominantly sidelined as they preferred to treat philanthropy rather than impact investment as a solution. Many impact investment projects were subscale, had thin margins and remained dependent on the support of impact investors throughout their life cycle. There was a need to broaden the definition of impact. It was not sufficient to confine the term to the bottom of the pyramid. Impact investment had to go mainstream to attract more funds from mainstream financial institutions, local High Net Worth Individuals (HNWIs) and retail investors.

The flip side of the coin was that ESG funds, often derogatorily called "impact investing on steroids", were presented by mainstream finance as a solution to the problem of scalability of impact investment. The ESG funds are based on the premise that rating publicly traded companies in terms of adherence to ESG criteria, yielded better outcomes. By adopting the ESG criteria, the mutual funds sector would create a virtuous cycle – the "good" ESG-abiding companies would have access to more capital, in turn more companies would adopt best practices in ESG. This utopian vision of ESG soon clashed with the reality of "greenwashing" – companies abiding by the set of ESG criteria to prevent harm in certain areas were engaging other activities that harm the nature or society, only to be "greenwashed" by the spin machine of Corporate Social Responsibility or Investor Relations projecting an ESG-friendly company. By 2022, greenwashing became such a burning issue that both the European Union and the USA exchanges reacted by cancelling many funds from the ESG compliant list.

The tarnished image of the ESG compliance revealed the limits of scaling-up impact. How can we scale-up impact investing and at the same time become loyal to its core tenets and values? I came to believe that two new aspects had to be incorporated firmly in the impact investment world: the better use of technology as a force for the scalability of impact and rigorous

The tarnished image of ESG compliance revealed the limits of scaling-up impact. How can we scale-up impact investing and at the same time become loyal to its core tenets and values?

measurement of social and environmental impact. That led to the next stage of my journey that characterized the last three years since 2019: the set up of the venture building firm Zingforce Ventures, the venture capital firm Purpose Venture Capital and the impact ecosystem builder – Turkey's first impact investing advocacy platform Etkiyap.

How to contribute to the world of purposeful investments?

One of the surprising elements of a journey is the seemingly unexpected turn of events. The occurrence of the coincidence per se does not determine the outcome of our journey – it is how we react to a coincidence when the coincidence presents itself and we make decisions based on how ready we are to embrace what the coincidence offers.

Since leaving Insitor Partners in mid-2020 I have participated in creating three new businesses. A venture-building and advisory firm, Zingforce Ventures. A venture capital company, Purpose Venture Capital. And a Turkish advocacy platform, Etkiyap, which literally means 'create impact'.

In the same way that my invitation to join Insitor manifested itself, all three occurred through grasping opportunities when they appeared. Zingforce grew out of a request from a

start-up to help them raise funds. We have since worked with an eco-friendly aquaculture firm in Korea, a supply chain platform for mom & pop stores in the Philippines, an electrification kit producer to convert scooter combustion engines into electric ones in Italy. The new VC business by teaming up with two remarkable professionals, Sharon Sim and Von Leong, who shared my vision on tapping HNWIs and Family Offices for the purpose capital market and, Etkiyap from a conversation with Safak Muderrisgil, at the Global Impact Investing Network Conference in Amsterdam in 2019 that has now evolved into a pioneering Turkish impact investing platform.

Photo by Giuliano Gabella on Unsplash

How to Embrace Change and Learn from Lessons

My journey is full of lessons learned. My key learnings will hopefully help those who would embark on a similar journey.:

- **Unlearn**. Jumping from the corporate world into entrepreneurship requires a lot more unlearning than learning. You need to have the right attitude to shed past habits, learnings and points of view and adopt a growth-minded, flexible, and agile mindset.
- **Seek partners who share your vision and values**. It is hard to find like-minded partners but once you get hold of them, build long-term alliances based on mutual trust and respect.
- **Define your purpose early**. Entrepreneurs, investors, or partners may have a difficult time articulating their purpose. Try to address the purpose as early as possible,
- **Invest in people, not excel sheets**. The likelihood of success of a venture is correlated to the strength of the team behind the initiative.
- **Be patient**. Building ventures with sustainability at their core is a vocation that requires a lot of patience and a lot of dedication. There are no shortcuts – you must be equipped for the long run.

Sertac Yeltekin is the co-founder and General Partner of Purpose Venture Capital, Singapore, (www.purposeventurecapital.com) and also the Founder and Managing Director of Zingforce Ventures, (www. zingforce.com) a firm specialized in venture building and advisory. He is also Deputy Chair of Turkish advisory platform Etkiyap.org Previously he held senior roles at Unicredit Group, and worked as a management consultant at Bain & Co.

By Roger Delves

The Value of Purpose

The role of values in the quest for purpose

If there is one thing that we look for and often find missing in our professional lives, many of us might agree that it is a sense of Purpose. Purpose is what should get us out of bed in the morning – though too often it is duty or obligation which do so. How then can we live lives that are purposeful? Perhaps understanding the concept better is a good first step.

Private purpose and professional purpose

Many of us have personal lives and professional lives that we tend to keep quite separate from each other. We may or may not feel we have a sense of personal purpose, but if we do feel we have such a thing, our personal purpose is something we create for ourselves, and we own. We do not inherit it and it cannot be delegated to us or imposed on us. If it does not come from within us then it is not purpose but may be obligation, and while we may well do many things out of a sense of obligation, as a driving force that sustains us obligation has nothing like the same power as purpose.

Changing purpose

Just as we own our sense of purpose, so we can change it. And we do – our purpose can change as our life develops. Marriage, children, illnesses, injury, divorce, death – the litany of things that can divert us from our sense of purpose, or can leave us feeling newly purposeless, is disconcertingly long. Moreover, purpose left unattended is inclined to stall. Purpose needs maintenance.

We can have more than one driving sense of purpose: we can have professional and private purposes that drive us, and we can have a private sense of purpose around family and another around self. But we need to be aware that our sense of purpose will drive our decision-making, so if we do have more than one sense of purpose then we may find that from time to time (sometimes frequently) they are in conflict, and this can make decision-making fraught and stressful.

Purpose at work

Our work purpose is why we do what we do professionally. It guides us. Without a sense of professional purpose, we tend to be rudderless and to drift, our direction decided by external factors that are equivalent to tides and winds. Work purpose can and often does come from the organization that employs us – often wrapped together with other concepts such as vision, mission, and values. Some companies provide careful and nuanced 'purpose statements' that are the result of research and thought. In other cases, the purpose statement is no more than a handy soundbite. Work purpose can also be self-imposed, and indeed a sense of professional purpose may be

Our personal purpose is something we create for ourselves, and we own. We do not inherit it and it cannot be delegated to us or imposed on us

what takes an individual into a particular place of professional endeavour – a sense of purpose around the importance of civic safety may, for example, be the driver for an individual to join the police force.

Meaningfulness, safety and purpose

Meaningfulness is derived primarily from our sense of purpose. If my purpose is to be the very best parent that I can be, or to play the best part I can in alleviating the exploitation of child labour, or to contribute my best efforts to delivering sustainability initiatives that will help to drive positive climate change, or to help build the best local football league that supports and develops young talent in a socially deprived area, then that purpose will give meaning to my life. I will feel that what I do has some benefit and is of some use – my effort will have meaning.

It helps if there is obvious significance in the tasks that I must carry out – I want to feel meaning in what I do, rather than force meaning into it – and it helps if there is variety in those tasks, so that I am not doing the same thing day after day. If that variety can call on several different skills, then that is even better.

Without a sense of professional purpose, we tend to be rudderless and to drift, our direction decided by external factors that are equivalent to tides and winds

But in doing what I do to deliver that purpose I must feel safe to be true to myself – I cannot be purposeful if there is pretence in my self-presentation. So, whatever my true self is, my internal and my external self, I must feel free to be that person at work as I pursue my purpose.

Purpose and values

Personal and professional purpose, and my willingness and ability to drive towards my purpose, is linked to my sense of values. Understanding what we mean by values, and knowing what values are and what role they play in our lives, helps us in turn to explore and understand our sense of purpose.

The work of Milton Rokeach, an American academic who researched into what we mean by values, is useful here to offer clear definitions. In his 1979 work, *Understanding Human Values* (Free Press) Rokeach defined values as "strongly held prescriptive or proscriptive beliefs about ideal **modes of behaviour and end-states of existence** that are activated by, yet transcend, object and situation." First it is important to note the subjective nature of values – they are "prescriptive or proscriptive" so they are limiting or restricting subjective beliefs. These beliefs are activated by "object and situation" – that is to say, by what we see and by situations in which we find ourselves – but these strongly held subjective beliefs transcend these situations, overcome these objects and dictate our actions by limiting our behaviour to be in line with these beliefs.

Here's an example: I might have a value – a strongly held prescriptive belief – that living a carbon-neutral life is critically important. That ideal end-state of existence transcends object and situation, so I can't, with this value, take long unnecessary trips alone by car, or drive when I could walk or cycle, or take avoidable commercial flights, for business or for pleasure.

Values are powerful things to have and when one person's, tribe's or nation's values clash with another's, the consequences can be severe.

Next, it is useful to explore further what Rokeach means by end states of existence and modes of behaviour.

Rokeach used the expression Terminal Values to describe values that captured end states of existence that we subjectively simply found to be highly desirable. So desirable that we were prepared to dedicate our life's efforts to achieving them. These Terminal Values tended to be of two kinds.

One kind was what could be described as self-regarding and focused on the way we wanted life to be for ourselves and our loved ones. Examples of such Terminal Values might include family security, inner harmony, career success, deep reciprocated love, social recognition, prosperity, or wisdom. Immediately we see that what for one individual might be a Terminal Value may for another be simply a desirable outcome or may even be something beneath consideration. It is also important to ensure that what we recognize as Terminal Values are our own Terminal Values and are not the ambitions or expectations or obligations that others may have for us.

The other kind of Terminal Value we could hold is described as other-regarding or selfless and describes a strongly held belief about an end state of existence that we want to help achieve. Examples of these might, alongside a carbon neutral footprint, also be reversing the progress of climate change, improving public health or education, elimi-

It is only for our Instrumental Values that we will die in a ditch or lie down in traffic

nating leukaemia or abolishing child slavery, or building a world free of discrimination, or ensuring national security for your country of birth.

Once again, the list can be endless, and what might be a Terminal Value for you may be someone else's mild interest. But what is again immediately apparent, and what we will return to, is the link between Terminal Values and a sense of purpose.

Instrumental Values, meanwhile, capture those behaviours that we subjectively feel to hold more worth or value for us than any others. Now here the list of words truly is endless, and what might make my list may not get anywhere close to your list. Contenders might be words like compassion, loyalty, dedication, precision, punctuality, courage, hard work, freedom, understanding, creativity or any of hundreds of others. Whatever your Instrumental Values are, they may capture behaviours that are no more than at best preferred behaviours for someone who on the surface looks exactly like you. Then of course there are what we recognize as rewarded behaviours – those behaviours that our organizations or our loved ones or our teammates reward us for holding to be important. Understanding exactly what my own Instrumental Values are, and what merely represent rewarded behaviours, preferred behaviours or perhaps required behaviours is very important.

Authentic leadership is leadership where a course of action is decided not by situational imperatives but by reference to an examined, broadly unchanging template of core values

Because it is only for our Instrumental Values that we will die in a ditch or lie down in traffic. We will, when the going gets tough, turn away from all the others and behave in a way that is contingent on the situation – doing what seems best in the moment. That is the power of our true values: we hold to them regardless of situation or circumstance. We act in a way that is congruent with them whatever the cost. These Instrumental Values represent our authentic selves.

It is often the case that there is a link between our Instrumental Values and our Terminal Values. I behave in certain ways because that behaviour helps me to move towards my Terminal Value – my end state of existence that I simply feel is more important than any other. So, for example I am courageous because courage is required to name discrimination for what it is, wherever it is found. My Instrumental Value of courage helps me to deliver my Terminal Value of rooting out discrimination from my society. Or I am conscientious because that helps me to live a carbon neutral life.

Purpose, values & authenticity

I want to return to the link between purpose, values and authenticity. I have shown, I hope, that my personal Termi-

nal Values (of which there should not be more than three or four) give my life purpose. These Terminal Values are likely to encompass some self-regarding end states of existence that capture the sort of life I want to live, and some selfless end states of existence that address more the sort of things in which I want to be engaged. My professional sense of purpose may be self-imposed, in which case it is likely to be expressed through personal values that I hold around my professional activities. Or it may be generated by the company that employs me having a purpose statement, one that engages me and that I find gives me a sense of professional purpose. Often, of course, I may bring my own sense of professional purpose, captured in a Terminal Value, to an organization where the attraction of the organization is that its purpose and mine appear to be aligned.

Now, if I am in a leadership role, I know that people both in my team and in the wider organization, will be looking at me and searching for reasons to be led by me. One of the biggest enablers around leadership is authenticity. People prefer to be led by someone who they find to be authentic. Michie and Gooty (2005) refer to Bass and Steidlmeier (1999) and to

Luthans and Avolio (2003) as they suggest that authentic leaders "are said to engage in self-transcending behaviors because they are intrinsically motivated to be consistent with high-end, other-regarding values that are shaped and developed through the leader's life experiences." The literature consistently tells us that authentic leaders have examined their values and identified those which are core. Luthans & Avolio (2003) define authentic leadership as leadership where a course of action is decided not by situational imperatives but by reference to an examined, broadly unchanging template of core values. George (2004) points out that to become authentic, each of us must develop our own leadership style, consistent with our own personality and character.

Luthans and Avolio (2003) see in the authentic leader a "seamless link between espoused values, behaviors and actions...building the moral capacity of leaders to make selfless judgements". This places values at the heart of an objective, a codified code of conduct which will lead to predictable and consistent behaviours and ensure that authentic leadership can have no egotistic intent.

The authentic leader's focused route to achieving the team or organization's objective must be one which encompasses an altruistic concern for others. George & Sims (2007) definition of authentic leadership describes authentic leadership as following one's own beliefs with courage and conviction whilst serving others, being genuine and pursuing personal growth. May, Chan, Hodges and Avolio (2003) say that authentic leadership is ultimately about the leader knowing him or herself and being transparent in linking inner desires, expectations, and values to the way they behave as leader every day, in every interaction.

Knowing oneself and being true to oneself are therefore the essential qualities of authentic leadership.

So, where does all this leave us?

Finding ways to be more purposeful and, if you are a leader, finding ways to help people in your team to be more purposeful must be a good ambition. We know that people with purpose are more *engaged*, and we know that more engaged people make for *better performing teams*. We also know that people prefer to be led by those whom they believe to be authentic, and that central to our idea of another's authenticity is our sense that they are in some way led or driven by values that are worthwhile and broadly speaking selfless. So, revisiting the Rokeach understanding of values – that we have Terminal Values that describe end states of existence that we pursue most avidly, and Instrumental Values that describe the behaviours that we value above all others – may well help us as leaders to be able to guide others towards a sense of purpose (especially, for example, if we lead within a coaching culture) and therefore increased authenticity.

A fully referenced version of this article is available. Please email **editor@dl-q.com** *if you would like to receive one.*

Educated at Oxford, **Roger Delves** *is a Fellow of the RSA and Professor of Leadership Practice at Ashridge, the executive education campus of Hult Business School. He is a member of the DLQ Advisory Board.*

By Amy Bradley and
Katherine Semler

Re-discovering Purpose in the Face of Overwhelm and Burnout at Work

Reports of chronic work stress appear in the press almost every day, with people describing themselves working longer hours, facing higher workloads and dealing with more demands at work and at home than they have ever known before. One recent study from Chicago Booth School of Business and others, on remote working found that working hours are 30% higher than before the pandemic, with over half of those additional hours being done outside the normal working day.

Recently, the American Psychological Association reported that 79% of people had experienced work-related stress that month alone. Moreover, research spanning 46 countries during the pandemic suggested that 89% of people feel their work life is getting worse, with 85% of them saying their

50% of the working population now describe themselves as over-extended at work

overall wellbeing has declined. Job resignations in the United States in 2021 were up by 15% on 2019, which was a record year in itself. Gallup's most recent State of the Global Workplace report suggests 80% of the working population across 155 countries are disengaged, with this lack of engagement costing the global economy $8.1 trillion each year.

Furthermore, negative emotions among employees, such as worry, stress, anger and sadness have now reached record levels, with 7 in 10 employees describing themselves as struggling or suffering, rather than thriving, in their lives overall. 50% of the working population now describe themselves as overextended at work, suggesting they may not yet be in burnout but without remedial action, may soon be on their way.

At a time when questions of viability and sustainability are becoming critical for companies, it could be argued that the growth and prosperity sought by organizations are dependent on ever-increasing pressure on employees to produce more and more, so the pursuit of unbridled growth must be kept in check by the fact that organizations are only as sustainable as their people. Overwhelm, exhaustion and burnout are pervasive among leaders and workers alike because of the nature of workplaces today. Burnout can be defined as a mismatch between expectations and reality when it comes to a person and their job. This mismatch may be – driven by workload (e.g. having too many targets and deadlines combined with not enough resources to do the job); control (e.g. being micromanaged or feeling a lack of autonomy or influence); reward (e.g. not feeling valued, appreciated or fairly rewarded for our efforts); community (e.g. feeling isolated from others, or experiencing instances of interpersonal conflict, disrespect or incivility at work); fairness (e.g. experiencing discrimination or favouritism); and values (e.g. continually being asked to do work that appears pointless, or experiencing a disconnect between our own values, motivations and ideals and those espoused and demonstrated within the organization).

In our own research on the topic, we suggest that burnout persists because of an enduring work ethic that either leads us to believe that purpose and total engagement in our work is a measure of self-worth; or through a 'labour of love' work ethic, where many people mistakenly look to their work for fulfilment, friendship and even love. In this vein, perhaps one of the reasons burnout continues unabated is the emphasis we place on the role of work in our lives. We mistakenly look to our work as the source of all our fulfilment – "a means not just to a pay cheque but to dignity, character and a sense of purpose." Burnout persists because we cling to these ideals and fear losing the meaning that work promises. It is only when we reassess the relative importance of work in relation to other aspects of our lives that we can begin to address burnout.

We know from our research that there is a point at which wanting to do a good job becomes bad for your health. Studies have also shown that we can have too much of a good thing when it comes to our relationship with work. For example, identifying with a particular group or team at work can satisfy our innate desire for belonging, bringing us much-needed social connection and support. At the same time, a strong sense of belonging can act as a primer to push us to work harder, take on more responsibilities and help colleagues even if not formally requested to do so. It is our motivational drivers,

It is only when we reassess the relative importance of work in relation to other aspects of our lives that we can begin to address burnout

We have a responsibility as individuals to notice and recognize the disconnect as it emerges between our aspirations for work and our lived experience of work itself

such as our need to feel valued and our need for social bonds, that become the very things that can lead to overwork, even workaholism. Overcommitted employees have been described as having "difficulty withdrawing from work – continuously striving for high achievement because of an extreme need for approval and esteem from work."

To truly tackle burnout, not only do we need to challenge societal norms and expectations concerning work as the source of our purpose in life, but we also need to pay attention to the organizational environments we find ourselves caught up in. While those employers who are concerned about addressing burnout can take steps to improve the conditions of work, we also have a responsibility as individuals to notice and recognize the disconnect as it emerges between our aspirations for work and our lived experience of work itself. We understood from those who have contributed to our research that some people find themselves so dependent on their work as a means of self-worth that they become unable to detach, despite becoming increasingly dissatisfied with their day-to-day experiences of work. Some of our co-contributors talked about having become so seduced by the material benefits of work, such as salary and status, that they felt unable to get out. Others talked about how the "promise" of reward and the metaphorical pot of gold at the end of the rainbow had kept them striving until the point at which they burnt out and could give no more. From the stories we heard, it is those people who acted with tough compassion who were able to save their souls. Tough compassion means being able to spot and surface our own (and others') unhealthy behaviours before it is too late. It means facing up to difficult conversations about the detrimental impact of work, and it means living with clearer boundaries between work and non-work in service of our long-term wellbeing. That said, tough compassion can take its toll when attempts at dialogue are dismissed or blocked. However, in the end, the decision to leave an organization is sometimes the most compassionate thing we can do for ourselves. As Elizabeth Svoboda writes, "Exiting from a harmful situation can be its own form of uncompromising truth-telling."

All our research co-contributors said they had all been profoundly changed by their experience of burnout, but through the experience, had been able to discover alternative purpose and balance that was more attuned to their needs and to the dangers that lie in excessive work. Many of them referred to knowing their limits better, communicating what they would and would not do, and shaping the work conditions they needed to remain whole. The people we spoke to described practices that had helped them to heal and to remain purposeful, healthy and self-aware in the face of demanding, high-pressure or intensely emotional work. Strikingly, all of these practices were embodied, meaning that our bodies and our physical existence are central features in these approaches. From the stillness of meditation to the explosiveness of running,

or the mindful physicality of painting and photography. If a central feature of burnout is that we lose much or all of our physical and emotional awareness of ourselves, then finding a restorative regular practice offers a powerful means of helping us find our way back to awareness and self-care.

If we are to make the changes required to tackle burnout at its roots, this cannot be achieved by individuals alone. We must also demand different working conditions, with employees and employers co-creating a shared vision of what it means to lead a healthy work life and of how work fits into a life well lived. Addressing the root causes of burnout may require wholesale system change, such as challenging the basis upon which we currently measure 'contribution' at work. It may require, for example, to move beyond time as the primary measure. As working professionals, many of us have become so anxious about justifying our time to clients, or demonstrating our use

"Exiting from a harmful situation can be its own form of uncompromising truth-telling."

and utilization to our employers, we even measure ourselves in terms of monetizable hours. It has been suggested that organizations should move to outcome-based work as a means of unshackling employees from the time–productivity equation. There may already be moves afoot in this regard, with over 10,000 employees worldwide trialling a four-day work week. But, despite widespread enthusiasm for shortening the standard working week, it remains to be seen whether this simply creates pressure on employees in different ways. If we are to radically reimagine a world without overwhelm, exhaustion and burnout, we would need to see organizations where compassion for self and for others is prioritized, even at the expense of productivity and companies that are as concerned about collective wellbeing as they are about profits. Workplaces that affirm purpose comes from leisure, not just from work would be the norm rather than the exception. If we are to truly tackle burnout, organizations need to be radically reimagined, so that routines and processes do not stifle and control; they become 'listening' systems in which people treat one another with unconditional positive regard and co-workers are strongly connected and in tune with each other's needs. We know from existing research that teams built on principles of reciprocity, for example, have increased cohesion, belonging, relational commitment and mutual trust. Furthermore, research suggests that in organizations designed around reciprocity – incorporating practices such as hiring for relational skills, using participatory selection processes, focusing on

Workplaces that affirm purpose comes from leisure, not just from work, would be the norm rather than the exception

group incentives and rewards, fostering relational meeting practices and using collaborative technologies – reciprocity becomes a virtuous and generative process, enhancing a sense of community and improving performance.

If we are to re-discover our purpose in the face of overwhelm and burnout at work, the answers not only lie at the doors of employers, but also belong to us as individuals. To move towards improving our broken relationships with work, work should play a part, but not the whole part, in bringing purpose to our lives, with us deriving meaning from other domains such as our hobbies, volunteering activities, community work, families, friendships and creative endeavours and this must happen collectively with each of us holding one another to account in ways that honour our health, dignity and our humanity.

A fully referenced version of this article is available on request.
Please email **editor@dl-q.com**

Dr Amy Bradley *a Professor of Leadership and Management and author of 'The Human Moment'. In 2020, she was named on the prestigious Thinkers50 Radar of global management thinkers. She contributes as adjunct faculty at several leading business schools. She is co-author of 'Running on Empty: Navigating the Dangers of Burnout at Work'.*

Dr Katherine Semler *works with leaders and organizations to help them define and live their purpose. She is a senior partner at global consulting firm, Korn Ferry and adjunct faculty at Ashridge Hult International Business School. She is co-author of 'Running on Empty: Navigating the Dangers of Burnout at Work'.*

By Rebecca Stephens

The Power of Purpose

"For scientific endeavour, give me Scott; for swift and efficient travel, Amundsen; but when you are in a hopeless situation, when there seems to be no way out, get on your knees and pray for Shackleton." **Sir Raymond Priestly**

The above quote is from the Heroic Age of Antarctic Exploration: Roald Amundsen, the first to reach the South Pole, on 14th December 1910; Captain Robert Falcon Scott, close behind him on 17th January 1911, sadly to perish with his four companions on the return journey just 11 miles from a food depot. And Sir Ernest Shackleton, a man affectionately called 'the boss', who lived his finest hour over a century ago on the Imperial Trans-Antarctic Expedition of 1914-17—an expedition that spectacularly failed in its mission to cross Antarctica, but which Shackleton turned around to be one of the greatest stories of survival ever told.

His leadership is one from which many have drawn inspiration through the years, but which is particularly pertinent today, in our troubled times of conflict, economic hardship, and the ever-present existential threat of climate change, when, in our darker moments, we might easily believe we are in a 'hopeless situation' with seemingly 'no way out'.

Shackleton's story is a perfect illustration of how it need not be a constant – it can shift with life experiences and circumstances

Shackleton's expedition is well documented. His ship, Endurance, was stuck in the sea ice 'like an almond in a chocolate bar' before even reaching land, and his 27-strong crew was trapped nine months on the ship. Then, when the unimaginable happened and the ship was 'crushed like matchsticks' before their eyes, they endured a further five months camped on the ice, until, finally, the thaw released them into the open sea and they rowed—frozen, wet and mad for thirst—for seven days, to Elephant Island, a small, dark outcrop of rock jutting from the Southern Ocean. It was relief, surely, to be on terra firma, but still they were a very long way away from any shipping route. Shackleton then took the biggest risk of his life and

with five men set sail in a 23-foot whaler, destination South Georgia, 800 nautical miles to the north and east, where they knew there to be a whaling station. The journey wasn't over even then. They landed on the wrong side of the island and three men out of the six still able to get to their feet climbed over unchartered peaks and glaciers to Stromness whaling station, and life. After immeasurable effort, Shackleton chartered a ship and sailed back to Elephant Island where all 22 of his crew awaited his return. Not a single life was lost.

There is an ebb and a flow to this story which many of us might relate to in our own lives, in which there was a sense of purpose—a meaning to the existence for Shackleton and his men—to be the first expedition to traverse Antarctica, which was then stripped away from them when the Endurance was trapped in the ice. Shackleton and his crew were stuck for weeks that stretched into months, through the long spell of darkness of the Antarctic winter, literally 'at sea', unsure of their direction, whether the ice might thaw and enable them to continue their quest, or not.

It is perfectly okay not to know one's purpose, for periods of time.

That uncertainty ended with the sinking of the Endurance. Shackleton's hopes, dreams and ambition to be the first to cross Antarctica were dashed. 'I cannot write about it,' he said, but in the same instant his purpose—his reason for being—was restored: to survive, and to get his men home alive.

Purpose, knowing why we do what we do, adds meaning to our lives and might be considered an anchor to our well-being. Shackleton's story is a perfect illustration of how it need not be a constant—it can shift with life experiences and circumstances—and is different for different individuals. 'Polar exploration is at once the cleanest and most isolated way of having a bad time which has been devised,' wrote Scott's companion, Apsley Cherry-Garrard. It is certainly not for everybody. Although interestingly, despite the suffering, and the heart-breaking loss of friends, Cherry-Garrard looked back at his time on the ice as the most important and enriching of his adult life, in large part because of the camaraderie—more of which anon.

For now, suffice to say that a sense of purpose cannot be faked. It bubbles from within. It requires knowledge of self and often courage to follow one's true path. And it is perfectly okay not to know one's purpose, for periods of time. We are all familiar with the teenager who fails to see the point of putting in the effort at school; the middle-aged man who is made redundant; and all too often, people in full employment. Once the mortgage is paid and food put on the table, there are many jobs that fail to satisfy. One woman I worked with declared that her friends considered her the most 'successful' of their entire social group, but that she was unfulfilled and deeply unhappy.

Lacking purpose can lead people to question their identity and self-worth even in the most comfortable of circumstances. During those long winter months on board the Endurance, there was in addition a constant shadow that they might not make it home alive. It is worth mentioning, perhaps, that it was far from unusual in this era for expeditions to crumple under the strain of isolation in the these most extreme of environments. For expedition members to be lost to starvation, scurvy, or exposure, and for people to dissent, fall into depression, even commit suicide. Yet not only did every one of Shackleton's crew survive, but to read their diaries is to learn that the majority were, for most of the time, happy.

So how did Shackleton do it? How did he hold everyone together and keep up morale when the opposite seemed much the most likely? First, the nature of the man cannot be ignored. He was both compassionate and optimistic—the latter a characteristic he upheld above all others. There is a degree of irony in that arguably it was an overly generous dollop of optimistic bias—a belief that bad things happen to other people, rarely oneself—that got him and his crew into the mess in the first place. Shackleton had been warned by Norwegian whalers in South Georgia that the ice floes were further north than they had seen in living memory, and that it would be prudent to postpone his expedition until the following year—but he set sail regardless. Today, we need to call upon that same optimism to work in our favour, to endow us with strength and vision to see through the darkness to a shaft of light the other side. Something Shackleton never lost.

Building trust and talking frankly and openly, were keystones of his leadership

Shackleton had many flaws, something he would readily admit of himself, 'yet,' he said, 'I hate to see a child suffer, or to be false in anyway', a quality others recognized in him as well. 'A Viking with a mother's heart,' is what his second-in-command Frank Wild called him. He learned compassion through personal suffering, ill health, and homesickness as a young apprentice in the Merchant Navy and was far from being a fan of the rigid, hierarchical order of the day. His style was less formal. Building trust and talking frankly and openly, were keystones of his leadership. In today's parlance he might have been regarded as a guru in emotional intelligence. 'There are a lot of good things in the world, but I'm not sure that comradeship is not the best of them all,' he said. For Shackleton, teamwork was more than an ingredient for success; it was a goal in itself.

When the Endurance was well and truly wedged in the ice, Shackleton didn't outwardly display the slightest disappointment. Rather he spoke to his men calmly, told them what must have seemed obvious, that they must winter in the pack ice, explained its dangers and possibilities, remained optimistic and prepared for winter. The best Shackleton could hope for was that the ship would withstand the polar winter and be freed in the spring thaw. Meanwhile, the men found themselves without a job, and Shackleton's role, as leader, was to find a way to tackle their crushing disappointment, boredom, and fear, and sustain a shred of hope that the ship would indeed be released, and they would continue their journey.

More than anything, he dreaded the effects of boredom on a crew with no responsibilities or routine

The most important message, surely, is that of empathy, connection, and compassion

More than anything, he dreaded the effects of boredom on a crew with no responsibilities or routine. His answer was to maintain structure, for the crew to feel secure. Set meals and Saturday night sing-alongs. Ordinary duties maintained, as closely as it were possible on an immobile ship. To fill the vacuum, he ensured each man had challenging and meaningful work, even if the work might not have been considered a priority in the normal run of events. Harry 'Chippy' McNish, the ship's carpenter, for example, was asked to make furniture for a hut yet to be built at a future base camp (still hoping their mission was only delayed); the scientists among them were set to collecting specimens from the ice and studying atmospheric, ice and water conditions; while training the dogs became something of a sport.

He was also a stickler for a nutritious diet and exercise in the belief, as is evidence-based knowledge today, that physical and mental well-being are inextricably linked.

Perhaps the most important lesson from Shackleton, though, in these troubled times, is the deep understanding and empathy that he had for his men. For Shackleton they were not just staff, but fellow human beings. He invested tremendous effort in developing personal relationships with each one of

Launching of the James Caird on its rescue mission from Elephant Island to find help, aboard, Sir Ernest Shackleton, Tom Crean, Frank Worsley, John Vincent, Timothy McCarthy and Harry McNish Photo taken 24th April 1916

them, even with those with whom he had little in common. He loved his books, kept the ship's library in his cabin, not only for his own pleasure but also to read up on subjects that were of interest to others, so that he might always have a point of conversation. He was particularly concerned as the Antarctic winter drew close, the sun to set and not rise again for a further four months. For many it was their first experience of such a long spell of darkness, and he took pains for them to be in the right frame of mind. His was always an open-door policy, listening to his men's concerns and keeping them informed about the ship's business.

He was also remarkably sympathetic of the stresses and strains and odd little obsessions that showed themselves. On the Endurance, there was a character, Thomas Orde-Lees, who by all accounts irritated everyone with his surly, condescending manner and selfishness. He became obsessed with the possibility of running out of food, and if food items went missing,

It seems unlikely the crew would have held it together without Shackleton, but equally Shackleton needed the crew

they would invariably be found squirreled under his pillow. The crewmen grew only more irritated, but Shackleton, generally tolerant of people's quirks and foibles, put him in charge of the food store and in so doing successfully allayed his anxieties.

There is so much to learn from Shackleton's approach, for those supporting a friend or colleague who has lost their way, or who feels adrift themselves. Make sure to have structure in your life: regular meals, exercise, enough sleep. Find some meaningful work, even if it is not true to your core. Stay calm—questioning one's purpose is natural, maybe even necessary—and optimistic, that if it is your wish, if you explore the world around you while staying true to yourself, you will find a powerful purpose. But the most important message, surely, is that of empathy, connection, and compassion. We are primarily social beings. We exist in relationships with others, and it is our commitment to these relationships which is the deepest and most motivating force. This is so obviously apparent with parent and child, but reaches beyond, to the wider family, friends, and community. Not to forget our colleagues at work as well—human beings do not stop being human when they walk through the door into the office. It was Shackleton's love of his men, his determination that not a single life would be lost, that empowered him with the strength to endure, to stay positive, to take the toughest of decisions, and ultimately risk all and sail the most audacious of journeys, 800 nautical miles across the Southern Ocean to South Georgia in a tiny little wooden boat, the James Caird, now forever recorded in the annals of polar exploration.

It seems unlikely the crew would have held it together without Shackleton, but equally Shackleton needed the crew. In the literal sense, McNish the carpenter shored up the James Caird to withstand the violent storms of the Southern Ocean, and there is little chance they would have safely reached South Georgia without Frank Worsley's remarkable navigational skills. But it was the very fact that they were there that really mattered, to have another human being for whom to fight.

To take for granted the motivating power of the bond between us as human beings is to very seriously miss a trick; it fails to acknowledge who we are and what is our reason for being – our purpose – and the productivity that arises from this truth. The more difficult the challenge, the more important it is for us not to turn inward, but to reach out to those around us, to forge friendships, to act for others as well as ourselves. Then we are committed; then we have purpose. It is only through recognition that connection is where our deepest energy lies that we can hope to resolve the economic crisis, the gaping poverty gap, and climate issues we face.

Rebecca Stephens MBE. First a journalist for the Financial Times Group, then a mountaineer (first British woman to climb Everest and the Seven Summits), Rebecca is the author of books, lecturer and coach on the human face of leadership.
enquiries@rebeccastephens.com / **www.rebeccastephens.com**

Join our **online session** *with Rebecca on February 28th where she will be discussing* **Shackleton and Purpose** *with DLQ editor Roddy Millar.*
developingleadersquarterly.com/current-events/

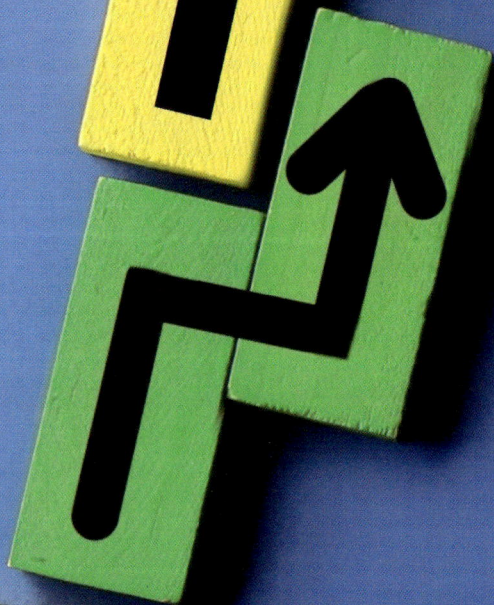

By Beliz Ülgen

The Chair Effect

Its implications for organizations

In many organizations, the promotion process is not always managed under fair conditions. Why is this?

There are a variety of reasons. Often it is due to an organization not building the correct association between the requirements of the position and the qualifications of the employee. In some organizations the qualifications and the characteristics of managerial candidates are not taken into consideration in the performance evaluation process. Sometimes it is due to not using the appropriate performance evaluation methods to measure the employees' achievements or failures fairly. In their evaluation, organizations may prefer one-sided (manager-subordinate) evaluations that are likely to be subjective or biased rather than receiving feedback from different actors (peers, customers, suppliers, team members). Still too often, too many organizations use unfair promotion approaches such as nepotism, favouritism and cronyism.

Too many organizations use unfair promotion approaches such as nepotism, favouritism and cronyism.

As a result, employees who are promoted do not have the mindset and appropriate leadership capacities to carry out the responsibilities of the position and manage their relations with others—often changing their attitudes and behaviour negatively towards colleagues when they become a manager. This negative change occurs due to the newly acquired managerial position and is what I call the 'Chair Effect' (The chair being one of the major symbols representing managerial positions).

In this article I introduce the phenomenon of the 'Chair Effect' and outline how organizations can avoid it happening. It is based on research with colleagues across a range of different industries. This qualitative research was conducted with twelve professionals who have directly experienced a manager's behaviour and attitudes pre – and post-promotion.

The research points to the chair effect being caused by three types of factors:

- Individual factors (hubris syndrome, power, personality, and sense of revenge)
- Organizational factors (organizational culture and role models)
- Contextual factors (country culture and social environment).

Employees who are promoted often change their attitudes and behaviour negatively towards colleagues when they become a manager. What I call the 'Chair Effect'

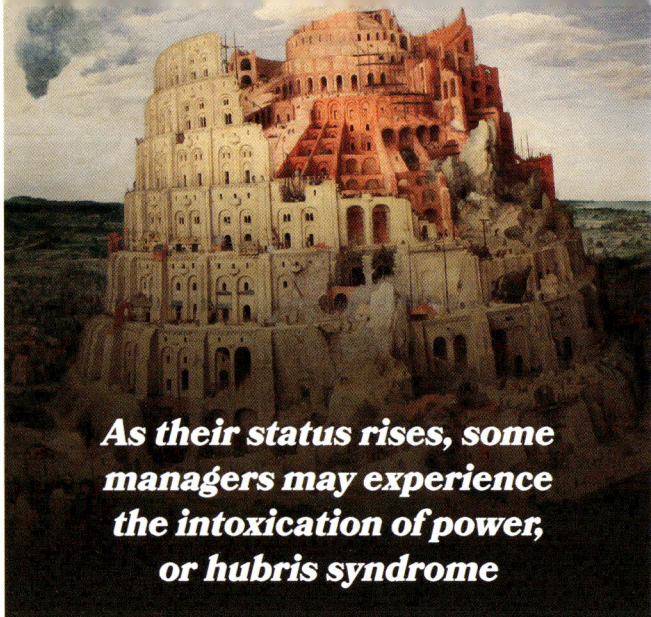

As their status rises, some managers may experience the intoxication of power, or hubris syndrome

Individual factors

Hubris syndrome and power

Coming from Greek Mythology, the term hubris means exaggerated self-confidence or pride. The three basic factors that cause hubris in work settings, are having a high degree of power, reduced limitation in using authority, and the length of time that the managers/leaders have been using this authority. Hubristic managers consider their abilities, performance, physical and mental characteristics superior to those of others, and they accept others as average in comparison with themselves.

When individuals get promoted to managerial positions, their positions in the organizational hierarchy may influence their use of power and the degree to which they are affected by power. As it is known, although it changes depending on the sector and scale of the organizations, there is a significant difference between the position of the department manager and the general manager in terms of the field of power that they cover and the opportunities they offer. As their status rises, some managers may experience the intoxication of power, or hubris syndrome, by being adversely affected with all the advantages of that power (such as managing more subordinates, having more influence in the decision-making process, earning a larger salary, having a larger office or more luxurious executive car, etc.) and they may easily get caught in the Chair Effect.

In our research, hubris syndrome was observed particularly in managers who were promoted to upper-level positions (such as C-level executive positions: CEO, CFO, CIOs. V-level executive positions: VP, SVP and D-level executive positions: Director of Sales, Director of Finance).

Personality traits

According to the research results, personality traits are seen as the premier reason why people get caught in the Chair Effect and the two concepts related to personality traits are emphasised by the participants. One is the mature/immature characteristics and the other is dark traits.

The maturity characteristics such as being independent, active, having a high level of self-awareness and control or immaturity characteristics, including being dependent, shallow interest in job content, and having a short-term perspective are essential parts of personality when they are associated with the Chair Effect. As employees' personality traits mature, they can cope with the challenges of managerial positions better. But in some organizations, people become managers despite their immature characteristics. Immature characteristics are fertile ground for the symptoms of the Chair Effect to be seen

Some people hide their dark traits until they are promoted – then they exhibit narcissistic behaviours, competing with unethical methods, and belittling others.

Managers who have insufficient qualifications but are promoted only because of their good relations with their superior, or are on the same political side, get caught in the Chair Effect.

prominently. Another prominent theme related to personality is dark traits. Some people hide their dark traits until they are promoted but after the promotion they show these traits in different ways such as as holding their interests above others, exhibiting narcissistic behaviours, competing with unethical methods, and belittling others. These are classic behaviours that nurture the Chair Effect.

Sense of revenge

Among executive candidates, those who are exposed to the harmful effects of power, unfair management practices, and high levels of damage of self-interests may increase their revenge motivations. If an offender's damaging practices and behaviour are not dealt with by the organization, revenge comes to prominence as an unofficial solution by the victim. In some cases, the victim delays revenge because of the risks related to benefits such as bonuses, social interactions, company-paid lifeand health insurances, profit sharing, wellness support, etc.) and promotion opportunities that come from the organization. On the other hand the offender's position in the organization relative to the victim may strengthen, delay, or prevent the occurrence of the revenge. Offenders with high-status have more influence on victims than the ones at equal or low status. Due to this, sometimes, the victim waits until gaining at least the same power as the offender, and after achieving this he/she may experience the Chair Effect with this feeling of revenge.

Organizational factors

Organizational culture

In the interaction between organizational culture and employees, organizational culture leads, forms, and influences the employees' attitudes and behaviour. Therefore, mismanagement practices and negative culture can cause negative employee behaviour. In such organizations, some employees might consider mismanagement practices or negative behaviour as necessities for promotion. If a majority of the employees accept these wrong practices, it can lead to others in the minority group becoming influenced by these attitudes and behaviours and so try to copy them. Often this is done unconsciously.

Role model

Managers being positive role models may inspire employees by their personality traits, work-life principles and successes. Alternatively, positive behaviours can be generated by people who are the victims of negative behaviours from their bosses. It is possible that some people will be startled from these negative outcomes and determine not to make the same errors, so take precautions and show a tendency to do the right, legal, and beneficial things. Or, if the poor behaviours of negative role models are not punished, employees may perceive all these wrong-doings as acceptable and legitimate, and see advantages in behaving like their negative role model managers. As a result, the employees who are affected by negative role model managers may get caught in the Chair Effect more than ones affected by positive role model managers.

Unfair promotions, especially nepotism, favouritism, cronyism, and the lack of a fair promotion system within the organization were emphasized as other important drivers of the Chair Effect when we spoke to interviewees about the organizational factors that made most impact. Managers who have insufficient qualifications but are promoted only because of their good relations with their superior, or are on the same political side, get caught in the Chair Effect easily.

Contextual factors

Country culture

The Chair Effect can often be caused by the cultural values in which people grow-up. In this context, the chair effect is associated with three aspects (Individualism versus Collectivism, Power Distance, Masculinity versus Femininity,) of the six cultural dimensions of Geert Hofstede's cultural typology.

In highly individualistic countries, primarily north European and Anglo-Saxon cultures, there is a tendency to build weak relationships, and support individual achievement. In contrast, collectivism places much greater importance on group cohesiveness and shared responsibility. In individualis-

In individualistic cultures, solidarity is replaced by competition, and managers influenced by this culture can experience the Chair Effect easily

tic cultures, solidarity is replaced by competition, and managers influenced by this culture can experience the Chair Effect easily to protect their interests, pursue their achievements, and save their power and status.

In cultures with high power distance, there is a high degree of respect for authority, as well as an inequality of power distribution, dependency, less autonomy, and centralized decision-making. In organizations and institutions which have more hierarchical structures, the formal and power-oriented relationship between managers and subordinates is most often observed. In low power distance cultures, there is more equal distribution of power and authority, independence, autonomy, and low hierarchy. Managerial positions are not as concerned with status symbols. Decentralized decision-making, open communication, involved management approaches, caring equality and fairness are the other main characteristics of these cultures. People who most likely come from a low power distance culture will continue to focus on some basic concepts, such as equality, merit, talent, and expertise, after becoming managers. Whereas people who are influenced by the high-power cultures in which the intensity of respect increases in compliance with the degrees of power and authority, are more likely to experience the Chair Effect.

Our research shows that power distance is observed as a significant dimension of the Chair Effect. High power distance increases the privileges of managers against subordinates. It is observed that some of the managers who get caught in the Chair Effect used privileges negatively to protect their status and power and to show themselves as superior to others.

*One of the main reasons
for incompatibility is
improper and unfair
practices in the decision-
making process
around promotions*

Cultures with a high femininity ranking, display specific characteristics such as humility, social care, cooperation, sensitiveness to interpersonal relations, and concerning quality of life, in contrast to masculine cultures where power, materialist values, competition, not caring for other people, and ambition are more important than human relationships. We see that people who grow up under more masculine cultural environments, may be more likely to experience the Chair Effect when they are promoted to managerial positions.

Social environment

Social environment includes all the factors of immediate physical surroundings such as family size and family networks, wealth, education, social equalities and ethnicity/race. The characteristics of the social environment can influence the behaviour of people , and even their health directly or indirectly . In light of this research, the negative characteristics of the social environment where managers were born and grown up may also influence the Chair Effect.

A manager who has immature characteristics may display selfish or self-oriented behaviours towards their subordinates to preserve their chair or status.

Suggestions of how organizations can tackle the Chair Effect

For organizations to foster effective management not only depends on the achievement of organizational goals but positive relationship management with all employees. Good relations between managers and employees leads to success, collaboration, creativity, competitive advantage, and cooperation. On the other hand, incompatibility leads to many unfavourable outcomes. One of the main reasons for incompatibility is improper and unfair practices in the decision-making process around promotions. What can organizations do to avoid this?

I suggest six elements that can lessen the chance of managers being promoted into roles that they do not have the appropriate people skills for, and so reduce the risk of the Chair Effect occurring. The first three are already practiced in many organizations to varying extents, but a more consistent and comprehensive approach would bring wide benefits. The final three are perhaps less familiar, though easily implementable, offering opportunity to significantly and positively impact the promotion process, and making the Chair Effect a much rarer issue.

- First, there is a need to manage the promotion process fairly and evaluate meticulously the qualitative characteristics of candidates, such as their personality traits and their success in relationship management. This is in addition to quantitative characteristics, such as their performance score and relative seniority. Observation-based information should also be taken into account. Besides how well they get along with their peers, clients, or superiors, their attitudes and behaviours in conflicts and tense moments should be observed and noted.

- Second, although it is not reliable nor sufficient on its own, feedback from different actors regarding the candidates should not be ignored. Especially for managers who manage a large group of subordinates, it may not be easy to make comprehensive observations of their subordinates. For this reason, feedback of all the actors with whom the subordinates communicate and work together are helpful elements in a manager's evaluation. 360-degree Performance Evaluation can be a useful method for providing feedback to employees communicating with many different actors and especially working in departments such as sales, marketing, and corporate communications.

Implementing a probationary period of at least one year after promotion may be useful in observing the possible Chair Effect risk

- Third, in the evaluation process observing manager candidates through assessment centre practices is useful to obtain clues about their qualitative characteristics. For this reason, their participation in these practices should be observed carefully and evaluated. The content of all these practices – such as role-playing scenarios and group work – should be arranged in a thorough way for observing the candidates' qualitative characteristics.
- Fourth, careful management of those with immature characteristics. A manager who has immature characteristics may display selfish or self-oriented behaviours towards their subordinates to preserve their chair or status. They tend to build immature relationships that are based on closed communication (e.g. rarely conducting face-to-face meetings with subordinates, often interrupting others when they are talking, listening to what they are saying without caring) and lack of socio-emotional sharing (e.g. displaying non-empathetic approaches, not concerning or recognising if someone is sad, supporting competition-oriented relationships instead of social

interactions) in the workplace environment. Organizations have an important effect on the transformation of these characteristics into mature ones. It is not easy for employees to develop their immature characteristics in organizations where central authority, rigid rules, and fear culture dominate. Organizational cultures where employees have more autonomy, independence and creativity have more opportunities to develop their immature characteristics into mature ones.

- Fifth, implementing a probationary period of at least one year after promotion may be useful in observing the possible Chair Effect risk and preventing any possible negativities. Just as a probationary period is applied for newly recruited employees, this period should be implemented for managerial positions. It is assumed that as the rank of the position increases, the risk of the manager getting caught in the Chair Effect may be high due to reasons such as having more power, managing more subordinates, or having more financial packages. For this reason, the probationary periods can be extended as the seniority of the position increases.

- Lastly, the inclusion of the Chair Effect in the training and development activities of an organization will increase awareness amongst employees about its negative effects. This should include mentoring and management processes as well as career development training.

Beliz Ülgen is Head of Business Administration at Istanbul Ticaret University and has been a Visiting Professor at Grenoble Ecole de Management. She specialises in organizational behaviour and human resource management.

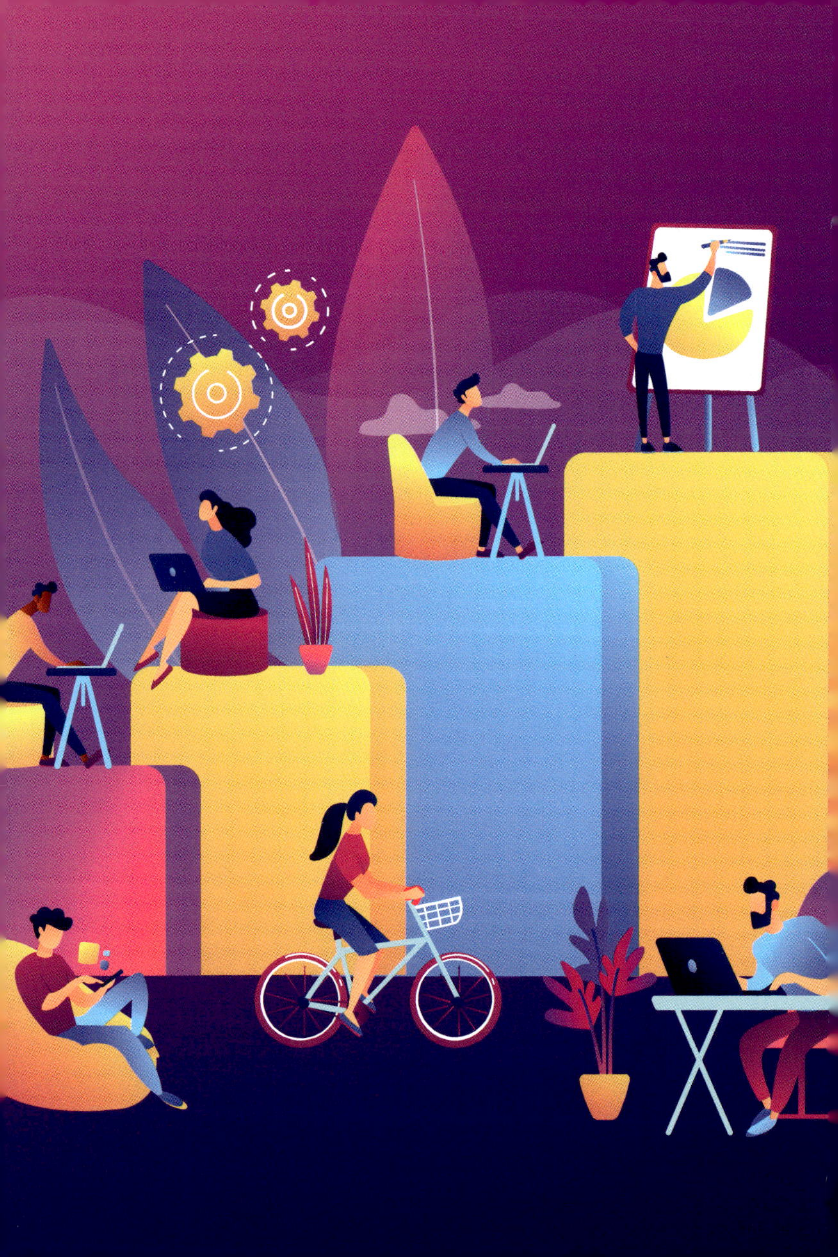

Yasmina Suleyman Halawi

Keeping Up with Millennials

"Millennials will comprise more than one of three adult Americans by 2020 and 75 percent of the workforce by 2025."
Morley Winograd and Michael Hais, Brookings (2014)

One of the most influential outcomes of the Millennials' entry into the workforce has been the way they have reshaped workplace dynamics and particularly our understanding of work-life balance in the face of performance-driven job environments.

In the past, work and life were regarded as separate yet co-dependent entities; people worked in order to live. Nowadays this does not hold true for the younger generation of workers; they do not see a clear separation between work and life; they see both as interdependent facets or one entity that pertains to their overall quality of life.

For instance, if they were to be asked the famous enigmatic question of "do you work to live or live to work?", they would be more puzzled by the question itself. For Millennials, it is neither; they want to love what they do and live while loving what they do for a living. They consider work as part of their personal identity and a way to living their lives.

Millennials want to love what they do and live while loving what they do for a living. They consider work as part of their personal identity and a way to living their lives

Workplaces and subsequently leaders who do not recognize this new integrative attitude towards work-life balance, are more likely to face higher turnover rates for their Millennial employees.

According to the US Bureau of Labor Statistics, in the wake of the pandemic, more than 47 million employees quit their jobs in the US, and as of 2021, the average national turnover rate reached 57.3%. Research by Pew Center found that Millennials (adults between the ages of 18-29) were more likely to quit than any other age group, with 37% voluntarily leaving their jobs in 2021.

The fact Millennials not only consider but also act on voluntarily leaving their jobs is an important factor in disrupting traditional workplace power dynamics, between employers and employees. Employees and Millennials in that sense can be considered to have become the key stakeholders in an organization.

Accordingly, it becomes imperative for organizations to address their demands and cater to their needs to keep them from voluntarily leaving their jobs.

So what can employers do to retain and keep up with Millennials? Is it only a matter of work-life balance?

Many of today's companies have catered to the expectation of a better work-life balance for Millennials, offering them more vacation days, more flexible work hours and workdays, and some companies have even started offering remote working options, particularly in the wake of the COVID pandemic. Yet the turnover rates remain high for Millennials despite such efforts.

What the Millennials are demanding is much deeper than what practitioners have assumed on the surface as their reason for 'job – hopping', and consequently labelling them as a generation that is 'entitled', 'lazy', 'don't want to work', and 'want too many days off'. It is beyond wanting a better work-life balance after all.

Retaining Millennials who are voluntarily leaving their jobs requires creating environments and cultures that satisfy their psychological needs and facilitate self – integrated and intrinsic types of motivation in the workplace, by way of meeting their basic psychological needs of Autonomy, Competence, and Relatedness. Such that when managers and companies provide environments that facilitate self-determined behaviour and thereby intrinsic motivation, they are more likely to attract and retain Millennial talent.

Millennials' psychological needs

If we look at Maslow's hierarchy with a modern-day lens (see Figure 1) we notice that many of the Millennial generation's basic Physiological and Safety needs are considered satisfied to a greater extent, thanks to their hard working and safety-net providing parents and family structures. With their basic physiological needs satisfied, as a generation, Millennials have shifted focus on satisfying their 'higher-order' psychological needs, such as belongingness, esteem of feeling accomplished, and Self – Actualization of achieving one's full potential. This explains as

With their basic physiological needs satisfied Millennials have shifted focus on satisfying their 'higher-order' psychological needs, such as belongingness, esteem of feeling accomplished

to why the vernacular of Millennials is filled with higher order need's jargon such as 'finding meaning', 'having a purpose', 'feeling fulfilled', 'seeking growth and development', 'enjoying work', and so on along such lines.

Figure 1 Maslow's Hierarchy of Needs

Maslow, A. H. (1943). A Theory of Human Motivation. Psychological Review, 50(4), 370-396.

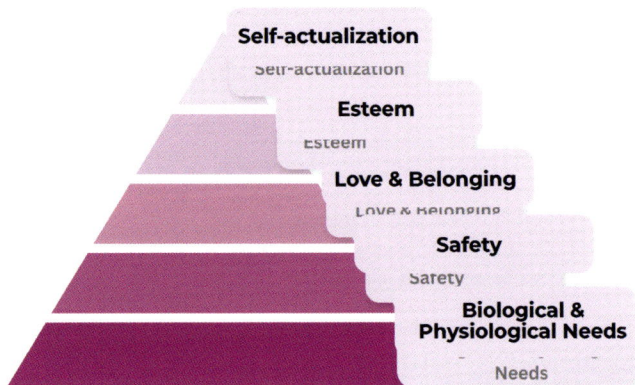

In that light, Millennials aim to fulfil their higher-order needs; they value and seek jobs and work environments that feel authentic, and congruent with the self. They are after performing tasks that feel self-integrated, and self-determined towards achieving their full potential. In the absence of such fulfilment, they are likely to leave and seek alternative jobs and work environments.

Creating environments that provide the structure for Millennials to feel 'whole' and 'true to self' in the work they do, can be done through establishing workplace cultures that satisfy their higher-order needs, such as Autonomy, Competence, and Relatedness. Although higher in order, these are considered the basic psychological needs required to yield positive behavioural outcomes, intrinsically-motivated, and self – determined behaviour.

Figure 2 Desire to Fulfil Need Leads to Internalization of Behaviour

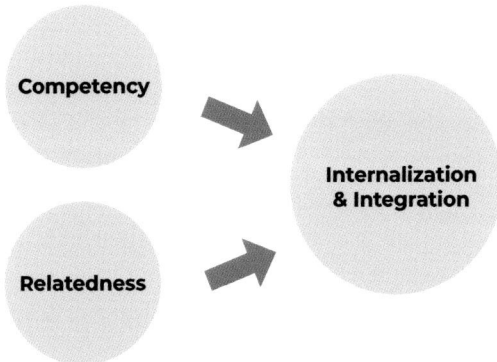

Creating environments that provide the structure for Millennials to feel 'whole' and 'true to self' in the work they do, can be done through establishing workplace cultures that satisfy their higher-order needs

Psychological-needs and enhanced motivation

The Theory of Self-Determination (SDT) purports that at the core of each individual is an innate tendency towards self-actualization; a desire to develop and grow psychologically. This desire translates into individuals wanting to take ownership in seeking experiences which they find expands their abilities and allows them to reach their potential, and at the same time they find rewarding and resonates with their sense of identity and belonging.

There are two ways in which individuals can experience tasks and behaviours as psychologically fulfilling, these are the Internalization of the behaviour or task and Intrinsic Motivation towards it. Both include the element of finding personal value and meaning in an otherwise externally imposed task or behaviour. This sense of meaning resonates with feelings of being 'true-to self' and reaching one's own potential.

Table 1 below explains the mechanism by which Internalization and Intrinsic Motivation enable tasks and behaviours to be experienced as psychologically fulfilling.

Once behaviour is either Internalized or the individual gains Intrinsic Motivation towards it, then that person begins to find personal value and meaning in their behaviour, they thus feel autonomous, competent, and subsequently they experience relatedness and belongingness towards their environment or workplace.

Table 1 Psychological-needs fulfilment mechanism

Internalization	A strive to integrate behavior that is externally imposed or valued by others towards finding personal value and meaning in performing it
Intrinsic Motivation	Having curiosity, Pursuit of Challenge, and Competence – Development Having an innate energy when pursuing an activity because it is fun or interesting

Source: Ryan & Deci (2017). Self Determination Theory, Basic Psychological Needs in Motivation, Development and Wellness. Ch.(8), 179-215

Accordingly, environments that facilitate these pathways (of Internalization and Intrinsic Motivation) will enable individuals to experience a sense of fulfilment and self – actualization that in turn leads to satisfying their psychological needs for Competence, Relatedness and Autonomy. This in turn will equip individuals with a sense of self that is aligned with the core of the person and feels authentic and intrinsically congruent with their values and beliefs. Thus, enabling them to experience autonomy to the extent they start to feel valuable for

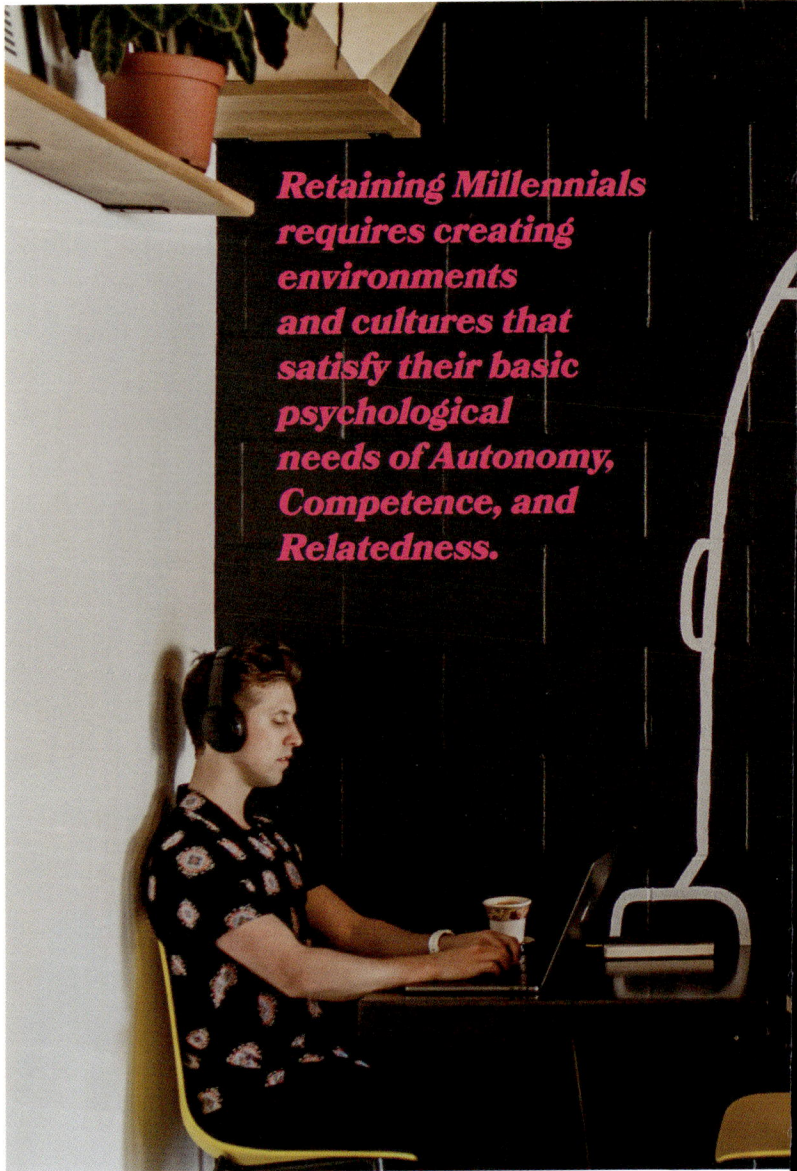

Retaining Millennials requires creating environments and cultures that satisfy their basic psychological needs of Autonomy, Competence, and Relatedness.

who they are as a person and not just for what they do at work (merely task-completion).

When a particular behaviour is a result of an experience that is fully internalized by the person, it is considered to be an intrinsically motivated behaviour.

The significance of Intrinsic Motivation

Intrinsically motivated behaviour is behaviour that is considered interesting by the person and brings them inherent joy and satisfaction, as opposed to being driven by a desired outcome that is extrinsic (such as pay and status).

Behaviour that is not fully intrinsically motivated can range on the motivation continuum from the lesser extreme of Amotivation (no motivation to act at all) to more internalized and thereby self-regulated degrees of motivation such as Extrinsic Motivation.

For behaviour to become Intrinsically motivated and fully autonomous, it has to become independent of external outcomes, such that behaviour is carried out beyond the reason of extrinsic rewards, but truly out of an innate drive for doing so. This is when behaviour is fully integrated with the self and fully internalized.

In Cognitive-Development practice this is referred to as Organismic Integration; in which the individual's behavioural response to their environment are integrated and internalized.

In the context of workplace job performance, Organismic Integration within the framework of SDT is said to occur when the employee operates from a place of feeling competent in their abilities, feeling connected to their peers, and feeling motivated beyond external control strategies such as rewards and pay. Overall, they are more likely to operate with an increased sense of ownership, full autonomy, and self – determination.

This sense of meaning resonates with feelings of being 'true-to-self' and reaching one's own potential

Rewards, Autonomy, and Intrinsic Motivation

According to research, as infants develop into toddlers and progress into childhood, their level of intrinsic motivation decreases; in a study that looked at children from third to eighth grades, with each increasing year the children's scores on curiosity, preference for challenge, and independent mastery attempts, were observed to decrease. In the framework of SDT, this is suggested as resultant from the societal environment in which parents and teachers use control strategies of behavioural motivation, such as evaluations and rewards. These types of controls are considered to elicit behaviour that is extrinsically motivated as opposed to intrinsically motivated behaviour (such as a student's innate curiosity and joy of exploration and learning). Even further, control strategies are linked to

When a particular behaviour is a result of an experience that is fully internalized by the person, it is considered to be an intrinsically motivated behaviour.

outcomes of thwarting intrinsic motivation where it existed to begin with; for example, setting deadlines for homework or in the case of a piano learning student, having her parents put her through piano examinations thwarting her fun and inherently joyful experience of learning how to play the piano.

The more an environment continues to impose such control strategies, the inherent joy for the act itself, such as knowledge exploration and play, or learning the piano slowly diminishes as children begin to lose sense of autonomy in carrying out the behaviour as a result of conforming to societal demands and expectations.

When behaviour is extrinsically motivated as a result of control strategies such as rewards, it tends to undermine intrinsic motivation, and is also found to be less autonomous.

Autonomy Leading to the Internalization of Behaviour

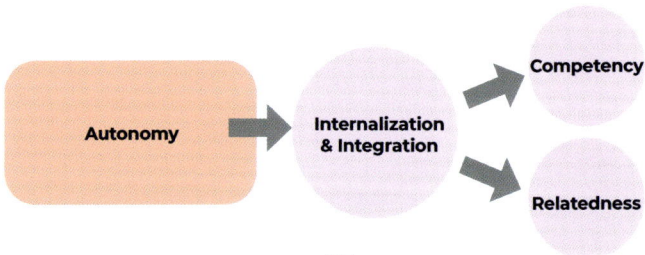

Meaning extrinsically motivated behaviour is also behaviour that is low in autonomy.

The more the behaviour becomes integrated with the self, the more the behaviour becomes aligned with a person's own values, beliefs, and becomes their own; thus, the behaviour becomes internalized.

An increase in internalized regulation of the behaviour leads to an increase in autonomy, as the behaviour becomes more self-determined by the individual. And the person begins to carry out that behaviour as result of autonomous self-determination.

Internalization and regulation of behaviour also enables individuals to feel competent and connected (related) to their peers and teams.

What does all of this mean for managers?

In order to keep up with the Millennials, managers need to create environments that facilitate Integrated Extrinsic Motivation and Intrinsic Motivation, and to adopt leadership styles that promote Autonomy, Competence, and Relatedness in the workplace. Indeed, this requires a major shift in organizational culture and leadership.

It means the best approach for keeping Millennials on the job is by motivating them on the job, which requires providing a combination of an environment that nurtures intrinsic motivation as well as one that supports higher-integrated forms of extrinsic motivation. This combination will yield a workforce that is more autonomous, more competent, and feels more connected (or relatable to each other), thereby satisfying their basic psychological needs.

Subsequently, their work attitudes and job satisfaction will increase, and ultimately will decrease turnover rates.

The nurturing of these psychological needs requires leaders to shift the focus on the individual as a unit of organizational well-being instead of the firm at large.

For example, Servant Leadership is a leadership style that is individual-focused and aims to satisfy employee's needs and development. Servant Leadership is an offset of Transformational Leadership with the distinction of the latter's foci being on the organization as the unit of development instead of the individual.

A Servant Leadership culture encompasses the practices of listening, awareness, stewardship, empathy, healing, commitment to professional development, conceptualization, foresight, persuasion, and the building of a community.

Such elements in leadership style of Servant Leadership indeed provide the needs-satisfaction of Autonomy, Relatedness and Competence.

A few companies have adopted this approach and incorporated it into their work culture elements to nurture Autonomy, Competence, and Relatedness in their work environments.

*A fully referenced version of this article is available on request. Please email **editor@dl-q.com***

Yasmina Suleyman Halawi *is an internationally certified advanced self-development and leadership coach based in Washington, DC, currently completing her Doctorate with a research focus on context-specific leadership development and coaching as a tool for developing leaders. She is a Fellow at the Institute of Coaching at Harvard McLean Hospital, contributing to research projects in the field of coaching and also the founder of jazzycoach.life, delivering Millennial and Intergenerational focused ExecuLife Coaching.*

Happy Hits!

by Spotify • 5,116,842 Likes

SHUFFLE PLAY

FEATURES

Yasmina Suleyman Halawi

How Spotify Keeps Up with Millennials

An example of an organization that has successfully created an autonomous workplace is Spotify, the commercial music streaming service company. Spotify switched its software development process from Scrum to Agile, with the belief that Agile principles of cross-functional teams working on full product development cycles mattered more than the Scrum practices of roles and responsibilities assigned for each part of the product development process; and accordingly, they switched their leader's titles from Scrum Master to Agile Coach; shifting their focus from Master leader to Servant leader, creating a culture of Servant Leadership in the process.

Additionally, Spotify renamed their core organizational units from 'teams' to 'Squads' with autonomy as their driving force; they became known as 'Autonomous Squads'.

Autonomous Squads are cross-functional self-organizing teams with less than eight people, without an appointed leader; they have end-to-end responsibility on product life cycles;

They switched their leader's titles from Scrum Master to Agile Coach; shifting their focus from Master leader to Servant leader, creating a culture of Servant Leadership in the process

design, deploy, maintain, operations, and delivery; essentially all the product development parts. Each Squad has a long-term mission that they work towards, and they decide how to get there.

These Squads decide what to build, how to build it, and how to divide the tasks amongst themselves. The parameters in which the squad's Autonomy operates includes Squad Mission, Product Strategy, and quarterly discussed short-term goals. These parameters are important for Spotify's culture, and they are used as instruments of Alignment; a concept reiterated concomitantly with Autonomy. Spotify's culture is therefore one of high Alignment and High Autonomy, and it is widely accepted within their organizational culture that "alignment enables autonomy".

Another concept that is advanced in the culture of the company is that of Accountability; members of squads and squads overall are held accountable for their deliverables. They do this however with the support of receiving clear expectations, transparent strategies, and long-term vision connecting to their purpose as guidance and direction in completing projects.

The office space is optimal for working teams; almost all walls are white-boards; each Squad has their own space in the

office, with separate areas for working desks that are moveable, and screens that are easy to adjust to share with fellow squad members, and a separate lounge area for 'planning sessions'; as well as a 'huddle room' for smaller meetings or for quiet time.

According to Spotify, Autonomous Squads has made them work faster, by making decisions happen faster locally, and their employees have become better at their work as result of experiencing higher motivation. Squads are aligned on the over-arching vision of the company and they work towards that vision without compromising it by their independent squad goals; the catchphrase at Spotify is "be autonomous, but don't suboptimize – be a good citizen in the Spotify ecosystem".

It is likely that Spotify is capable of promoting both highly Identified and Integrated types of Extrinsic Motivation, as well as Intrinsic Motivation for some, as they genuinely and inherently happen to enjoy the work they do.

Spotify is a company that grew globally yet still managed to maintain its start-up feel culture, with autonomous teams and room for creativity and innovation, and empowerment— the type of environment most Millennials enjoy working within.

Squads are also exemplary of a team unit wherein Competence and Relatedness needs are secured (Self-Determination Theory). Each squad-member assumes a role and task in line with their own expertise (competence) and contributes to the functioning and achievement of its overall Squad objectives. As each squad-member experiences the impact of their contribution towards the completion of assigned projects, they further experience enhanced squad-synergy towards a shared vision. The dynamics of working in unity towards a common goal creates a sense of belonging and identification (relatedness) amongst squad-members.

"Spotify is probably one of the best places I have worked for so far. I have high regard for the team I had the opportunity to work with. The company has an amazing work culture with a good work life balance." Anonymous Spotify Employee on Indeed.com

Spotify's Autonomous Squads concept may sound like the perfect work culture for Millennials, right? It shall come as no surprise then that the founder and CEO of Spotify, Daniel Ek, is a Millennial, born in 1983. Moreover, Millennials make up the larger portion of Spotify's employee demographics, with only 14.1% of its workforce being over the age of forty.

As of February 3, 2023, Spotify's net worth is estimated at 23.42b, with 8605 full time employees, and a global user base of 456m, of which 195m are premium subscribers. Spotify is currently the leading platform for music streaming services, followed by Apple Music (88m users).

An examination of employee feedback and reviews of the company's culture and their experiences in working for Spotify, on websites such as Glassdoor, LinkedIn, Indeed, and Teamblind.com, revealed findings in support of mostly positive experiences. The overall theme from employee feedback indicates Spotify is a company that grew globally yet still managed to maintain its start-up feel culture, with autonomous teams and room for creativity and innovation, and empowerment—the type of environment most Millennials enjoy working within.

In a presentation entitled 'Building a Strong Engineering Culture' by Kevin Goldsmith, who was the Vice President of Engineering at Spotify between 2013 and 2016, he described Spotify's culture with the following characteristics:

- Learn from failure
- Innovation at every level
- Iterative development
- Agile-first
- Data-driven
- Autonomous teams
- Continuous improvement
- Shared responsibility
- Transparency
- Trust
- Servant Leadership

Spotify's leadership style and focus on autonomous teams and innovation is one that nurtures intrinsic motivation

This set and combination of characteristics is what defines Spotify's 'start-up' feel culture that is liked by Millennials. The last point openly addresses the type of leadership advanced by Spotify's culture as that of Servant Leadership. As such, Spotify's leadership style and focus on Autonomous teams, and innovation is one that nurtures intrinsic motivation and supports higher-integrated forms of extrinsic motivation. By way of satisfying its employees' need for Autonomy first, as depicted in Figure 3 in the previous article, Competence and Relatedness are subsequently satisfied.

Spotify has further engrained its culture's attributes into its 'Agile a la Spotify Manifesto', which has evolved into a cultural artifact as it is now printed on the walls of its offices. This manifesto serves as the company's set of values, as explained on the **Spotify Labs website**.

In an internal survey across Spotify's offices in Stockholm, New York, Gothenburg, and San Francisco, employees were asked to rate the following statement: "I really enjoy working at Spotify! I look forward to going to work on Mondays, I have great colleagues, and it's a great place to work".

The overall average rating in responses was 4.48/5. This rating can be considered a good indicator of overall level of satisfaction "I enjoy working at Spotify!"; and a positive indicator of motivation on both personal and group levels "I look forward to going to work on Mondays, I have great colleagues" ; and an overall approval of its culture "it's a great place to work."

They allow and encourage new fathers to take six months paid paternal leave. This particular policy has had the effect of generating up to 20,000 job applications per month.

Similarly, on comparably.com, 84 % of the polled Spotify employees said "Yes" to the question of "Do you look forward to interacting with your co-workers?". When asked "Are you typically excited about going to work each day?", 73% said "Yes."

Spotify's culture has managed to maintain its people at its core; this is known and felt in the way the company reiterates and reinstates its culture in the form of its artifacts and policies. For example, they allow and encourage new fathers to take six months paid paternal leave and provide for returning new parents one month of flexible work options. This particular policy has had the effect of generating up to 20,000 job applications per month.

Also, the Spotify Code of Conduct Handbook for example, stipulates all functioning requirements of an organization in alignment with capturing the essence of its culture and its flat non-hierarchical structure.

Another form of reinstating this is the focus on hiring the right talent to fit and maintain the culture. As can be found in the examination of numerous employee feedback and reviews by Spotify employees who advise those interested in applying or those who are in the process of interviewing to "show how they fit the culture", and that they are "a team player". One employee said "the cultural interview and fit is weighed heavily throughout the process (basically we don't want assholes who won't want to work as a team, regardless of engineering talent)." Feb. 24, 2018.

This employee's bold statement is demonstrative of Spotify's strong commitment to its culture and a work environment that supports it.

According to Goldsmith, firing is also as important as hiring in order to protect the culture. He also states that when Leaders provide direction and guidance and then they get out of the way, that is what makes a good engineering culture. Reinstating Spotify's commitment to an Autonomy supportive and empowering culture.

When Spotify employees were asked "how is the culture?" on teamblind.com, their answers included some of the following reoccurring words: "family", "fun", "social spirit", "celebrating achievements", "relaxing and fun", "supports learning", "autonomous", and "sense of belonging."

Indeed, Spotify's HR Blog proudly states that they embody a culture that is inspired by Self Determination Theory, hence their autonomous culture; emphasis on sense of belonging and teamwork and learning and development. All of which fulfil the needs of Autonomy, Relatedness, and Competence, respectively. According to Spotify's HR Blog, this type of culture is believed to empower, support, and drive employees to achieve the mission and vision of the company while remaining motivated throughout.

Autonomy is a central pillar of Spotify's flat non-hierarchical organizational structure.

Accordingly, Spotify has embedded it into its culture in three main actions: the autonomous ways the employees are responsible for their own and others' learning and development; in how they get to achieve their vision and purpose (they

One employee said "the cultural interview and fit is weighed heavily throughout the process (basically we don't want assholes who won't want to work as a team, regardless of engineering talent)."

decide how to get there, and are motivated by the freedom in finding ways of doing that); and in the individual's personal mastery in what they do both as individual and as the company at large to grow and develop.

"Great culture to learn and grow in. You have autonomy over your career and they emphasize on driving your own development." Anonymous Spotify Employee on Indeed.com

Spotify states that they provide the resources, tools, and support necessary for conditions of growth, development, and attaining purpose. There is no micromanagement but instead sharing direction of where the company is going, and the teams are responsible to decide for themselves how they get there.

The Learning and Development Team at Spotify is termed The Green House; they consider themselves gardeners of their greenhouse, a growth enhancing environment, that supports development of the individual and those around them; each person responsible for their own learning and they are expected to learn from each other and teach one another. Autonomy is experienced on the learning and development level.

Whilst most employees enjoy the benefits of such a culture, there are some exceptions, such as the following employee's review on Teamblind.com, who stated "for the most part it is a cool place but does not have much structure or clear career advancement...in the beginning it seems good but the deeper in your career you go the more it starts to feel like a waste of your time and effort."

When Joakim Snuden, former Agile Coach at Spotify (2015-2017), was asked about "what is the best thing" and "what is the most challenging thing" about working at Spotify, his answer was "Autonomy" to both questions. There remain certain challenges worth exploring when it comes to a working culture where autonomy is a central concept. However, these remain beyond the scope of this article.

Nevertheless, overall, Spotify's Servant Leadership culture is capable of facilitating an environment that satisfies the Millennials' psychological needs of Autonomy, Competence, and Relatedness, thereby leading to the creation of Identified, Integrated and Intrinsic types of motivation. Accordingly, it is anticipated that the rate of voluntary turnover would be low for Spotify.

Notably, during the Pandemic, in early 2021, Spotify granted its employees the autonomy to "work from anywhere". This policy resulted in a 15% decrease in attrition.

The most effective work environment is one that facilitates and fulfils the psychological needs of Autonomy, Competence, and Relatedness.

What can we learn from the Spotify model?

1. Autonomy supportive structures such as Servant Leadership cultures and cross – functional Autonomous Squads lead to the satisfaction of not only Autonomy, but also the psychological needs of Competence and Relatedness

2. The more these needs are satisfied the more self-determined the behaviour for individuals feel, in this case the majority of the workforce being Millennials are experiencing higher autonomy and thus their work feels more self-determined.

3. As a result of higher levels of autonomy leading to employees feeling more self-determined in the work they carry out, they are also experiencing motivation that is more identified and integrated, as well as feeling intrinsically motivated as they inherently enjoy the work they do.

4. Keeping up with the Millennials requires a change in culture and leadership styles that nurture psychological needs of competence, relatedness, and autonomy and that also enhance intrinsic motivation in the workplace.

Implications

Organizations that are struggling to keep up with their Millennials leaving them, can benefit from evaluating the extent as to how much they are satisfying their Millennials' psychological needs of Autonomy, Competence, and Relatedness. Subsequently revamping cultures that fulfil these needs and as result improve behaviour that is Integrated and Identified, and ideally behaviour that brings inherent joy and satisfaction in carrying out by employees, hence achieving the ultimate level of integration and internalization, that of Intrinsic Motivation. A workforce that is operating with higher degrees of internalization of behaviour is more likely to stay with the organization than to seek alternatives and 'job-hop'.

The most effective work environment is one that facilitates and fulfils the psychological needs of Autonomy, Competence, and Relatedness.

Spotify's culture is an example of this effective combination of meeting psychological needs and enhancing Integrated and Internalized types of motivation that has contributed towards their 'Millennial attracting' culture. A brief search on Twitter, Instagram, and LinkedIn of the company's famous hashtag #lifeatspotify reveals pictures and posts demonstrative of the fun and motivationally charged spirit at Spotify, which one also cannot help but notice the pictures and posts are significantly dominated by Millennials.

A fully referenced version of this article is available on request. Please email **editor@dl-q.com**

Yasmina Suleyman Halawi is an internationally certified advanced self-development and leadership coach based in Washington, DC, currently completing her Doctorate with a research focus on context-specific leadership development and coaching as a tool for developing leaders. She is a Fellow at the Institute of Coaching at Harvard McLean Hospital, contributing to research projects in the field of coaching and also the founder of jazzycoach.life, delivering Millennial and Intergenerational focused ExecuLife Coaching.

Marilyn Mehlmann

Lead for Satisfaction

Is it possible to lead in such a way as to maximize job satisfaction—for all? If so, why should we do it? And, can you have too much of a good thing?

Four dimensions of job satisfaction

One way to look at job satisfaction is to use a model derived from our physical needs. We are not only vertebrates, mammals, but also predators; this is a major determinant of our lives from birth. It means that we need four basic things:

1. Territory: access to sufficient resources for us and our dependents to survive
2. Community: access to support, especially when raising the next generation
3. Change: for predators, movement enables us to spot our next meal
4. Meaning: we are born 'unfinished' and need a way to impose meaning on what our senses tell us

The expression of each of these four needs is frequently criticized as hampering effectiveness in the workplace. We complain about territoriality, or 'turf wars'. We criticize 'cliques'.

We may believe that 'people resist change' (no matter what), and that looking for meaning in work is a waste of valuable time and maybe even dangerously new-agey. As usual, it's a question of balance.

Let's look for the balance: for healthy territoriality and community spirit, and pragmatic approaches to change and to meaning.

Healthy territoriality

Our need for territory comes with our backbone—all verte-brates have it. My territory needs to be big enough—just—to supply me with the resources I need for survival.

At work, having a satisfactory territory means having access to the resources I need to do a good job. (Such satisfaction seems, by the way, to be fairly uncommon.) When thwarted, we tend to compensate by reverting to physical territoriality. A visitor to a workplace can often 'smell out' territoriality. In places where great importance attaches to my seat in the cafeteria, my desk, my locker etc., you may surmise that employees are not satisfied with their access to the resources needed to do the job.

Territoriality is not only about physical resources but also, very much, about an inner conviction or feeling. When I begin to feel I can influence events ('agency', or 'empowerment'), my inner sense of territory expands. A strong feeling of agency makes me less dependent on external circumstances.

As a leader, if you address the inner territory of your staff, you may be sure that they will bring to your notice any deficiencies in physical resources without either fear or exaggeration. So, empowerment is a path to consider if you're coping with turf wars or apparently unreasonable demands for 'more'.

We are not only vertebrates, mammals, but also predators; this is a major determinant of our lives from birth.

Some potential actions for you to consider:

My own sense of agency: Leaders are regarded by others as powerful. Yet many feel so constrained by external demands that they see only one possible course of action. How are you?

Agree on clear responsibilities and success criteria: No-one should be in doubt, or misinterpret.

Being clear about success and failure is not the same as rewarding and blaming.

Ensure transparency and accountability: Being clear about success and failure is not the same as rewarding and blaming. It needs to be linked to personal development and support.

Establish clear processes: e.g., for sharing responsibility and defining success—also for budgets, planning, and making staffing and other personnel decisions.

Healthy community spirit

From herd instinct to team spirit

New-born humans are totally dependent on other people, to an extent unparalleled in the animal world. Our need for community is evident from minute one of our lives. We may speak derogatively of 'the herd instinct', but it is not only natural but essential for survival. The herd instinct tells us we need each other's support, that no-one can live a life in total independence of other humans.

An insecure manager may try to split-up a well-functioning group simply because s/he feels like an outsider. The manager needs to learn the value of community for getting results—and the group may need to find less challenging ways of expressing their sense of community. It is possible to build a team with a sense of We without falling into the trap of defining everyone else as Them; but because the us-and-them spirit is so much simpler, many times the path to a healthy, productive team spirit is ignored.

We may speak derogatively of 'the herd instinct', but it is not only natural but essential for survival. The herd instinct tells us we need each other's support,

Diversity and inclusion

Another aspect of community is coping with, and deriving benefit from, diversity and inclusion. Just consider gender. Men and women, and all the people whose sense of identity defies such binary categories, bring different strengths to your teams.

We know that, on average, males have a stronger territorial need than women. If you want empirical confirmation of the research, observe the behaviour of teenage women and men on buses and trains—you'll never again find a journey boring!

It is often asserted that women are more 'social' than men—once again, in general. If true, this offers a model for understanding otherwise odd facts of working life around the subject of promotion. Despite both rhetoric and action, there are still comparatively few women in higher management. But if promotion is interpreted as a means of expanding one's territory in return for sacrificing community, it makes sense. The person promoted is no longer 'one of the team'; and a woman who is promoted will find it harder to be accepted as a member of the community of managers.

If your staff seems to be more focused on out-perform-ing each other than on co-operating for the best possi-ble outcome, you may like to consider some ways to promote the sense of We.

Examine current incentives: Do you for instance still prioritize individual over team achievements? Do you encourage managers to find a balance between 'Theory X', 'Theory Y' and 'Theory Z' (McGregor, Ouchi) that best suits their teams, and to work towards more 'Theory Y'?

Whole person: Make it culturally acceptable to bring to the table not only questions concerned with the work, but also questions concerning the functioning of the team, and the individual's role. See for instance such methods as Fleck's Synergy or Open Space. (Tift, Fleck, Owen)

Non-judgemental communication: Encourage and enable non-judgemental discussion about what is important (values and visions) as well as about facts and decision options. (Mehlmann, Parry, Ziegler)

Flatter organization: Hierarchy can be seen as a way to institutionalize territorial boundaries. A more productive approach to organisation is to begin creating commu-nities. See for instance such approaches as Holacracy and Sociocracy.

Change

When people are exposed to extremely low levels of sensory input they quickly become disturbed—we quite literally need change, a physical need we have brought with us into our mental world. Boredom leads to physical as well as mental restlessness.

With this in mind, it may seem strange that so much is said and written about resistance to change, 'You can't teach an old dog new tricks,' and so on. But what is really strange is that we humans are as flexible as we are. Changes may hit us with about as much logic or predictability as the weather, yet time and again we adapt (and forget that it even happened)—though we may grumble and, at work, demand to be left alone to get on with the job.

Meanwhile, the pace of change is accelerating. Leaders are coping with unprecedented levels of external change. The burden can be eased if as many staff as possible are helped 'back' to an attitude that change is the norm. Designing and implementing change needs to be in everyone's job description, not the province of a few experts.

From this perspective, catering for productive change and innovation is not primarily a matter of planning, but of creating and maintaining a 'reasonable balance between dissatisfaction and hope', as noted by Warren Ziegler, Syracuse University, which in turn implies balancing creativity and stability: ensuring that the work environment feels safe enough and satisfying enough to take change initiatives, but not so safe and satisfactory that there is no perceived need for change. Remember to include yourself in the equation: is your balance sufficiently satisfactory that you can handle initiatives from your employees?

If you find yourself expending too much energy on trying to persuade or coerce staff to get behind necessary changes, you may like to consider:

Decision-making needs at the very least to be transparent and at best to be consensual – which is not the same as consensus. (Endenburg)

Anticipation, foresight, futures studies: the more people who can be engaged in futures studies, the more likely it is that both opportunities and risks will be anticipated. The crux is to define the context of the study: not so broad as to be meaningless in practice, not so narrow as to exclude all new perspectives. (Ziegler, Inayatullah)

Meaning

Is the search for meaning what differentiates humans from other animals? Viktor Frankl makes this claim, and maybe he is right, since we are born more 'unfinished' than most. Though who knows what goes on in the head of a dolphin?

Even pre-language beings begin life with a search for meaning, at least those born incomplete. At birth we have, unlike for instance insects, no idea how to interpret the constantly arriving, overwhelming quantity of sensory input. Our very first mental task is to find out what it all means. And with our transition to conversational beings, the search takes on a more abstract dimension.

Is the search for meaning what differentiates humans from other animals? Who knows what goes on in the head of a dolphin?

Many studies confirm the importance of meaning. Most of us would like to experience that our work has meaning. In the absence of any obvious meaning, we tend to invent one—or to make other people (children, parents, the boss, the destitute) carry the burden of our meaning, identifying as a parent, a philanthropist....

Industrial society invented the idea that employment as such might be the meaning of life—unthinkable even a couple of hundred years ago, when paid employment was regarded as a great misfortune to befall a free man.

If you sometimes doubt the meaning of your work, or believe that others do, you may like to consider the 'why' of it all:

How do you feel, on a scale? Do you find your work (and that of those you lead) totally meaningful, or meaningless, or something in between? How does that impact your own job satisfaction?

If this is the answer, what is the question? Imagine that the work you lead is the solution to a problem. Whose is the problem, and who benefits from the solution? Do you find these answers satisfying?

Extremes: It's possible to hold ambitions and expectations that are either too high or too low. Unrealistically high ambitions lead inevitably not only to dissatisfaction (which can be good,since it can be a trigger for positive change), but if predominant can lead to a lack of energy or will to prioritize. Working with values, visions and anticipation can be a way to set ambitions and expectations at a useful level. ( )

Inner Development Goals: If you are committed to the Sustainable Development Goals and/or to Corporate Social Responsibility, you may find it useful to review the Inner Development Goals and related material, to get a different perspective on ways forward. (IDGs, Cross-Cutting Skill Sets).The crux is to define the context of the study: not so broad as to be meaningless in practice, not so narrow as to exclude all new perspectives. (Ziegler, Inayatullah)

What's the verdict?

Why should we lead for job satisfaction?

It is possible to view this as a question of ethics (Harman, Österberg) or—at its most basic—as a question of human rights (e.g. NI direct).

Irrespective of ethical or legal issues, however, there is ample evidence that a workplace with high job satisfaction performs better than one with lower satisfaction. A reasonable hypothesis is that this effect will be most noticeable in a workplace subject to high turbulence in a context of high complexity—conditions that are likely to become increasingly common, given the current global situation.

Is it possible to lead in such a way as to maximize job satisfaction—for all?

Leading for satisfaction is not about striving to make everyone happy all of the time. It is about maximizing the possibilities for each person to find satisfaction in doing their work. It also allows for some malcontents: in every organization there will always be the equivalent of the farmer who complained bitterly about a poor harvest in a year of drought, equally bitterly in a year of floods, and who, faced with a season of perfect weather and bumper harvests, complained that the market would be flooded with produce, thus depressing prices to a point where it was hardly worth the trouble of going to market.

And, can you have too much of a good thing?

Indeed, as should be clear from the above, 'total' job satisfaction can become too cosy, killing the will and energy to initiate or participate in change. However, don't worry., it is not likely

Leading for satisfaction is not about striving to make everyone happy all of the time. It is about maximizing the possibilities for each person to find satisfaction in doing their work.

to happen. And if by chance it does – you know how to deal with it. Even the suggestion of reducing resources or breaking up teams should do the trick. Better yet, initiate conversations about ethics and meaning. There's always scope for improvement.

Territory, Community, Change, Meaning

Paying attention to these four elements in the leadership and management of teams can in itself bring about profound changes to the contexts they operate in, as well as deepening the attachment and commitment of employees to the organization. The intrinsic benefits fostered by such environments become compelling, and hard-to-replicate, encouraging greater employee productivity and retention through higher job satisfaction. And as a bonus: see your own job satisfaction grow.

Marilyn Mehlmann. Entrepreneur, co-founder of Legacy17, focused on 'people skills' for sustainable development. Combines psychosynthesis, empowerment and action research to co-create methods and tools for personal and professional development. Speaker, consultant, educator; author and co-author of numerous publications. https://legacy17.org

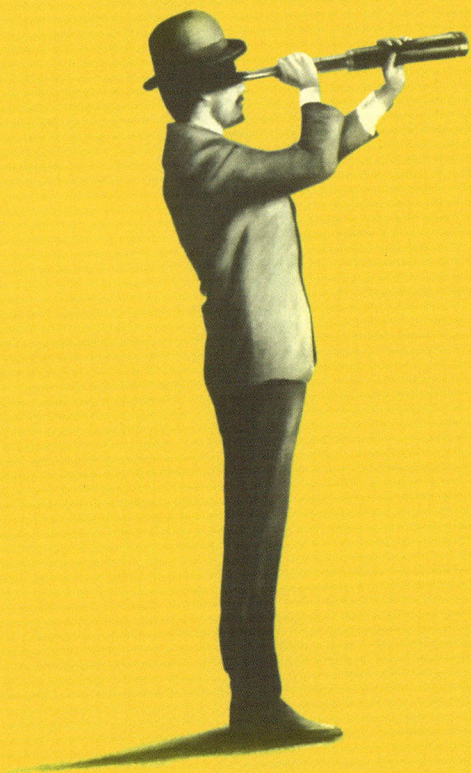

Organizational Curiosity RoundTable

Thursday 3rd November, 2022

Report by Roddy Millar

As publishers of Developing Leaders Quarterly (DLQ), Roland Deiser and I are driven by the opportunity to catalyze new ideas and thinking around leadership and organizational behaviour. We look to do this primarily through the curated and edited pages of this publication, where our contributing thought-leaders' ideas are presented after having been carefully crafted and distilled through the writing and publishing process.

Sometimes though it is important to shake-up that managed process with a less structured one – and so we also run online discussion panels with invited thought-leaders, where they can provoke each other's thinking and responses in an unscripted and more immediate manner. We shall be

Community is critical for curiosity, otherwise the benefits fail to scale

running several of these live sessions each quarter, to dig deeper into themes explored in the previous issue, with contributing authors and also new voices.

We ran the first of these online RoundTables in early November 2022 to delve into the cover topic of issue 39: The Curious Organization. The panel was hosted by Roland, with two of the article contributors from the issue, Novartis CLO and author of The Curious Advantage, Simon Brown; and our regional editor, the strategy consultant Saar Ben-Attar. You can read their articles in the back issue **here**. Simon and Saar were also joined by two new guests – Francesca Gino, the high-flying Harvard Business School professor, who also works with their Mind, Brain, Behavior initiative, and author of Rebel Talent; and Perry Zurn an associate professor of philosophy at the American University in Washington DC, and co-author of Curious Minds.

We were not disappointed – the conversation raced along. DLQ subscribers can watch the full session online at **developingleadersquarterly.com/past-events/organizational-curiosity-roundtable/** – but here are some of the key outtakes from the discussion.

The Curious Organization

Simon Brown's curiosity around curiosity was triggered by the Novartis CEO, Vas Narasimhan, arriving at the business and challenging its culture by leveraging Dan Pink's 'autonomy, mastery, purpose' approach, which Narasimhan evolved into his

It is much easier to spark curiosity outside the organization than to get people to be curious within their own organization

'inspired, curious and unbossed' triptych and then asking 'what does curiosity actually mean in an organizational context?'. It's about questioning, exploring, going where others have not gone before, asking things people have not asked before. It's about experimenting, seeing what works and what doesn't. And then learning from it.

For Perry Zurn the critical element of curiosity that makes it really valuable as a tool, is not the capacity to acquire new information, but the ability to connect. It connects ideas, but it also connects people, especially within an organization. Community is critical for curiosity, otherwise the benefits fail to scale. It also, as Francesca Gino, points out allows ideas to be viewed from different angles and perspectives, surfacing new information and knowledge in the process.

The panel all noted that curiosity is something we all start with as children, but it gradually gets eroded in most of us, by the structures of organization, either formal or informal. Francesca's research suggests our curiosity peaks at age four or five years old. Saar Ben-Attar underscored this with his statement that curiosity is an act of collective leadership. It is much easier though to spark curiosity outside the organization than to get people to be curious within their own organization. A useful trick to is try and connect those elements, see how the external curiosity that exists easily can be brought to spark internal curiosity.

Leaders tend to underestimate how much they influence those around them. If leaders are asking questions, it quickly becomes acceptable to do that, and others follow.

How do we institutionalize curiosity?

Spencer Harrison at INSEAD was quoted as pointing out that Google likes to learn from its new employees, those who have arrived from other organizations or cultures. Most often organizations like to 'onboard' new employees, to show them 'how things are done here', while that can oil the wheels for the new employee, it also dampens the value that they have and the new insights they can bring.

The culture issue cannot be underestimated, it is all-pervading. In Novartis, they measured differences in team capacities between teams with favourable and unfavourable ratings of their leader. The largest divergence was on curiosity. Those teams with favourable ratings were 22 points ahead on curiosity than unfavourable leader teams. If the leader is shutting things down, and controlling, the willingness to experiment and explore is hugely limited. Francesca Gino supports this, noting that leaders tend to underestimate how much they influence those around them. If leaders are asking questions, it quickly becomes acceptable to do that, and others follow. Much of the culture setting is actually very low-key, day-to-day behaviours. Francesca had researched a specialist US Airforce spy plane pilots group, and saw how the change in

behaviour of one influencer in the group, not the leader, triggered a greater curiosity across the group. It only requires one person to start this.

The Enabling Leader

This is all part of the shift away from the concept of the leader as someone who has all the answers, to the leader as someone who can bring the best out of a team. In a complex world the former is impossible, while the latter becomes ever more valuable. Creating a safe environment for asking questions is the skill needed. Start with 'I wonder if....?' type questions, as these require input from those around you. And push the boundaries. Don't ask ' how do we get 3% growth?' ask 'how do we get 300%?'. That creates the space for people to free-think.

Or as a leader say 'I'm here to learn, I don't know what the answer is – let's find it together'. The problem is that in organizations the act of exploring is often seen as time-wasting, as

> *The problem is that in organizations the act of exploring is often seen as time-wasting – that much of the exploration will unearth little – but you have to do that to find the gold*

much by the individual themselves as those around them. We need to shift that mindset to a longer-term one, which understands the benefits such learning can bring, and that much of the exploration will unearth little, but you have to do that to find the gold. It is those micro-moments where we dampen curiosity by saying 'we can't do that' rather than 'it seems out of reach, but how can we do manage that?'.

An approach Saar uses is to ask clients 'how they got here?', when 'here' is their current situation. Too often we do not explore these things, but when the question is asked of a team, you get as many different narratives as team members, and it is by unpacking those and understanding them that great insight is gained. And that curiosity to explore further is fertilized, and new connections are made. Perry Zurn builds on this idea, that too often we think of curiosity as searching out the new, but there is great richness in finding greater understanding from the past too. 'There are lots of ideas that are super-old, that would help us today', he explains. This is where community and ecosystems can be so valuable, in showing us ways to do things better, which they are already doing, rather than trying to be innovative and new always.

Making Leaders Curious in Practice

All this is well and good – but the fly in the ointment, is that new ideas are also an impediment. If you know how you want to do something, or have been doing adequately one way for a long-time, it is inconvenient and often tiresome to explore new ways to do it. How do we open up leader's minds to this, Francesca asks. Simon believes data is part of the solution. Gartner research indicates only around 25% of today's skills will be relevant in three years' time – we must keep learning to keep relevant. Data also shows that organizations with curiosity cultures perform better, Spencer Harrison shows a correlation between curiosity and long-term performance. It is vital to champion this data to build the culture as an critical business imperative rather than just a nice-to-have.

Curiosity may not be the word to use though – it may be better achieved if dressed-up as innovation or operational excellence or growth mindset even. And senior leadership needs to champion this all the time, reinforcing how important it is, and rewarding others for doing it.

Oops, I dropped the Lemon Tart

Roland wondered if we need to get more friction into the process to generate the innovation we seek and if that friction lies at the edges of the organization, rather than the safer spaces internally. For Saar the edges are fruitful places to explore, but leaders are often fearful of taking people to explore

We must keep learning to keep relevant – organizations with curiosity cultures perform better

there, as it seems riskier – in more full sight of others. But in his experience, people are willing to do this and enjoy it. Leaders need to be embrace this risk more. Often the risk can be in doing nothing – especially in fast-moving environments where everyone is seeking new processes. Understanding context can only come from exploring the boundaries, and this combined with an open mindset, often catalyzed by crises, as Francesca retells in the 'oops, I dropped the lemon tart' story. (You'll have to listen to the recording or buy her book for that one!). The lesson being around creating permission for people to embrace change and innovate has to be given, and seen to be given, for the culture to be sufficiently safe to live it.

There is always much more in a conversation than we can capture in a few pages, but we hope this brings a flavour of what the RoundTable surfaced and catalyzed. In the final 40 minutes of the 90-minute session, the conversation roamed further and dug deeper – with the addition of Markus Rettich who runs the senior leadership development programs for top management at Daimler, joining the panel from the audience.

Join us on March 6th for our next RoundTable on the Quest for Purpose with HBR professor **Ranjay Gulati**, consultant **Ralf Schneider**, Managing Director at Better Business, and **Sertac Yeltekin**, Co-Founder & General Partner at Purpose Venture Capital.

For more information and to register for a DLQ event visit **developingleadersquarterly.com/current-events**

IDEAS FOR LEADERS

Academic research in
accessible and engaging
bite-sized chunks

HOW TO TURN PURPOSE INTO PROFITS

KEY CONCEPT

Corporate purpose can give employees a sense that their work is meaningful. Whether such meaningfulness translates into better corporate performance is dependent on a number of factors. These factors include the clarity with which top management communicates the purpose, and whether middle managers and the company's professionals feel this sense of purpose and meaning.

IDEA SUMMARY

Milton Friedman notwithstanding, maximizing profit (and thus shareholder value) is no longer considered the one and only purpose of a corporation or business. The truly successful business is driven by a greater purpose that benefits society and our world and inspires a firm's leaders and employees by giving their work meaning. The inspiration and commitment at the heart of a purpose-driven company leads to greater profits: one does well by doing good. So says the common wisdom.

As often happens, what intuitively seems correct and logical is not always borne out in the real world. In short: do purpose-driven companies truly perform better financially than companies focused only on financial gain?

The challenge in answering this question is how to measure corporate purpose. Companies can have a wide variety of purposes — from saving the environment, to enriching the daily lives of the less affluent through less expensive, quality products and services, to providing innovative and affordable health care choices — to cite just a tiny sample. In addition, true purpose is much more than the pithy, easy-to-say words of mission and value statements. A slogan on a website and on marketing materials — our products make your lives better — is hardly proof of corporate purpose. As indicated by the definition above, true purpose is intangible — it is found in the hearts of leaders, employees and even customers. To measure purpose, you must look inside people, not read the marketing collateral.

A team of researchers from Wharton, Columbia and Harvard accepted the challenge of measuring purpose across a wide variety and significant number of companies and through a number of In conjunction with the Great Place to Work Institute, the researchers designed a comprehensive survey designed to reveal whether employees (not executives or marketers) had, as a group, a strong of the meaningfulness and impact of their work. Companies in which employees felt the meaningfulness and impact of their work were considered strong in purpose.

More than 450,000 employees across 429 firms participated in the survey over a period of six years. The survey questions came in the form of statements to which participants indicated — on a scale of 1 (almost always untrue) to 5 (almost always true) — whether the statement was accurate. Examples of statements on the survey included:

- "My work has special meaning: this is not just a job."
- "I feel good about the ways we contribute to the community."
- "When I look at what we accomplish, I feel a sense of pride."
- "I'm proud to tell others I work here."

The researchers then compared the level of purpose in companies to their financial results as measured by accounting (e.g. Return on Assets and Tobin's Q) and stock market performance. The results will disappoint some: the study showed no direct connection between corporate purpose and corporate performance.

However, a 'factor analysis', which is the effort to uncover relationships between purpose and other factors — revealed two categories of companies with purpose: the purpose-camara-derie company, which is the company that scores high on both purpose and workplace camaraderie; and the purpose-clarity company that scores high on both purpose and management clarity — that is, the clarity with which management expresses its expectations, and communicates where the company is going.

Workplace camaraderie was measured through survey ques-tions that explored employee perceptions on whether they considered their workplace a fun place to work, and whether there was a familial atmosphere among the employees. Clarity was measured through such survey questions as "Management has a clear view of where the organization is going and how to get there; "Management makes its expectations clear"; and "I am given the resources and equipment to do my job."

Comparing these two refined measures of purpose — purpose-camaraderie and purpose-clarity — to corporate results showed no correlation between purpose-camaraderie and superior financial performance. However, the factor analysis did uncover a correlation between purpose-clarity and finan-cial performance, notably in terms of future stock marketing performance.

The researchers further parsed the data from the data by divid-ing the results based on level in the organization, specifically: executives and senior managers, sales force, middle manag-ers, salaried professionals, and hourly workers. In general, the researchers found that the higher the level in the organization, the more likely the individual would believe that the company had a purpose.

In terms of relating purpose-clarity to financial results, the data showed that the perception of middle managers and professionals are what counted the most — that is, when middle managers and professionals believed in the purpose of the company, that company would show higher results.

BUSINESS APPLICATION

This study adds nuance to the pat phrase that a company "does well by doing good." Corporate purpose can drive higher firm performance, but the effect is far from automatic. Among the practical applications of this study are the following:

■ Executives tend to believe that the company has a purpose, but they should not assume that other levels of the organization share this belief. The company will want to make a targeted communication effort about the company's purposes aimed at the other levels of the organization.

■ Clarity is the required differentiator if the company wants to see its purpose reflected in the company's financial performance. Simply having a sense of purpose is not enough if the management has not clearly communicated its expectations and the direction and ambitions of the company.

■ Achieving buy-in into the company's purpose from middle managers and professionals is essential, for they are the employees who can translate purpose into performance

REFERENCES

Corporate Purpose and Financial Performance. Claudine Gartenberg, Andrea Prat & George Serafeim. Organization Science (January 2019).

Access this and more Ideas at **ideasforleaders.com**

IDEAS FOR LEADERS

IDEA #787

STAKEHOLDER VALUE: BEST FOR EVERYONE OR JUST POOR PERFORMERS?

KEY CONCEPT

Two academics argue that the current push for corporations to focus on nebulous stakeholder value rather than traditional shareholder value only provides cover for underperforming managers.

IDEA SUMMARY

In 2019, 181 CEOs signed a Business Roundtable Statement on the Purpose of a Corporation. The statement reflected a growing sentiment in corporate governance attitudes that the purpose of a corporation extends beyond maximizing shareholder value to maximizing the value for the benefit of all stakeholders—which according to the Statement include "customers, employees, suppliers, communities and shareholders."

The 2019 Statement replaced the Business Roundtable's 1997 Statement declaring that the primary objective of a corporation was to serve shareholders.

Critics of the shift from shareholder to stakeholder value argue that the concept of stakeholder interests is filled with ambiguity, including the challenge of measuring the value received by each stakeholder group, as well as the challenge of balancing the interests of each group. In contrast, traditional shareholder objectives are unambiguous: corporations know, by name, exactly whose interests they must serve, and the stock price metric of shareholder value could not be more precise.

A study by Ryan Flugum of the University of Northern Iowa and Matthew Souther of the University of South Carolina, based on corporate quarterly earnings announcements, highlights the issues related to the ambiguity of stakeholder value.

Quarterly earning announcements provide an objective metric of corporate performance based on whether companies met or failed to meet analysts' earning expectations. The study, based on an analysis of corporate communications in the two weeks following quarterly earnings announcements, including analysts' calls, quotes in news coverage, and discussions in analyst and investor conferences, showed the following:

- After quarterly earnings that fell short of market expectations, corporate executives were 34 percent to 43 percent more likely to emphasize their company's focus on stakeholder interests, using terms such as "stakeholder value," "the benefit of stakeholders," or "stakeholder interests."
- In contrast, after quarterly earnings that met expectations, corporate executives emphasized their company's focus on shareholder value rather than stakeholder value—even if in the previous quarter they had cited stakeholder value in explaining disappointing earnings.

The study also compared corporate earnings communications before and after the Business Roundtable statement, and found references to stakeholder value became 50 percent more prevalent after the Statement, notably in communications related to earnings that failed to meet expectations.

Finally, the study's analysis of CEO turnover figures following poor earnings performances found that executives who cited stakeholder value in earnings announcements were less likely to lose their jobs following announcements of underperforming earnings.

The study confirms the concerns of critics who believe the ambiguous metrics of stakeholder value maximization enables poorly performing managers to be evaluated more favourably.

BUSINESS APPLICATION

Leaders todays recognize that internal motivation — the kind The 2019 Business Roundtable Statement reflected a growing sentiment in the business and academic community that—in their own long-term interests as well as in the interests of their communities—corporations have a responsibility to create value for a wider group of stakeholders. These stakeholders include but are not limited to shareholders.

As Jamie Dimon, Chairman and CEO of JPMorgan Chase & Co. and Chairman of Business Roundtable, said in the announcement of the new Statement: "Major employers are investing in their workers and communities because they know it is the only way to be successful over the long term."

The Statement described stakeholder value creation, as "delivering value to our customers," "investing in our employees," "dealing fairly and ethically with our suppliers," "supporting the communities in which we work," as well as "generating long-term value for shareholders."

Critics, however, push back on the social pressure to replace shareholder value with stakeholder value in the objectives of a corporation, arguing that without clear, objective measures, stakeholder value objectives provide cover to underperforming managers and corporate executives. The end result, they argue, is management entrenchment.

This academically rigorous study highlights a sometimes-neglected truism: While attitudes and perspectives may evolve—gender diversity and sustainability are two examples of issues with which companies struggle today—management theories and prescriptions for success are never unanimous. Instead, they offer a pool of resources and information for study and consideration. In the end, leaders themselves must make the final decisions they think are best for the long-term success of their businesses.

REFERENCES

Stakeholder Value: A Convenient Excuse for Underperforming Managers? Ryan Flugum & Matthew Souther. SSRN Working Paper (November 2020).

Access this and more Ideas at **ideasforleaders.com**

THE ROLE OF IDENTITY WHEN AN ORGANIZATION'S PURPOSE CHANGES

KEY CONCEPT

How do organizations respond to multiple business logics with conflicting sets of rules and norms? New research based on a study of four French business schools reveals that institutional and organizational identities will guide an organization's response.

IDEA SUMMARY

Many organizations must deal with multiple 'logics' that come with different and often conflicting or competing rules of the game. For example, organizations in the medical field must balance the logics of science and care. Companies in the micro-finance industry balance commercial and development logics: they are bankers who are also involved in advancing developing countries.

What happens when a new set of rules suddenly take over your industry? The answer, according to a research team from French and Canadian business schools, lies in understanding your institutional and organizational identities.

The research is based on case studies of four French business schools dealing with two somewhat conflicting logics. The business schools are known as French Grandes Écoles de Commerce (FGEC). Until the mid-1990s, the rules of operation for FGECs were clearly laid out. For example, the credibility and cachet of a FGEC was the extremely competitive entrance exams, which made acceptance into a Grande École a high honour.

In the mid-1990s, however, major business schools became more and more internationalized. No longer did leading schools in different countries compete with their national counterparts. Instead, the competition extended to schools around the world.

The FGECs recognized that they could not continue to live in their insular world if they were going to attract the best and the brightest students from France and abroad and be relevant in the world of business academia. They had to adapt to the new International Business School (IBS) logics: for example, credibility now came from placement after graduation not stringent entrance examples; research was more valued than teaching; and international faculty with international PhDs were prized.

The institutional identity of each of the four French business schools in the study was crystal clear: all four were considered Grandes Écoles. However, at the organizational identity level — which refers to how organizations see themselves in comparison to other organizations in their category — there were some significant differences in terms of status and prestige. Two of the schools — ESSEC and ESCP Europe — were considered elite, stable schools among the Grandes Écoles, boasting strong GE programs. Grenoble EM was not as elite, but still had a 'respectable' Grande École program, while Euromed's GE program was considered poor.

The researchers expected that the four schools — and especially the two lower-tiered schools who were struggling to be considered a Grande École — would move away from the Grandes Écoles identity and adopt a clear International Business School identity. However, important stakeholders of the schools in France, including alumni associations, employers, the media, chambers of commerce and the Ministry of Education, wanted the schools to continue to sustain and nurture the tradition of the Grandes Ecoles.

At the same time, the schools had to react to the global dominance of the International Business School logic. For ESSEC and ESCP Europe, integrating an IBS identity would extend the elite status they enjoyed to the international level. Thus they made some changes to their GE program: ESSEC repositioned it as an MBA, while ESCP Europe added a European component. ESSEC, the only research-oriented school among the four, also continued its focus on research; ESCP maintained its emphasis on teaching but also recruited international faculty and research-oriented French professors. For Grenoble EM and Euromed, the IBS logic was a great opportunity to enhance and reconfigure their failing positions as major business schools. Both schools worked on becoming more research-oriented, including enhancing the capabilities of existing faculty and also recruiting international academics. Grenoble EM's chose a compartmentalization strategy, creating an international school within the school. Euromed, whose Grande École status was the most precarious, started from scratch, overhauling the school and eventually merging with the Bordeaux École de Management; it is known today as the Kedge Business School.

BUSINESS APPLICATION

The case studies of the French business schools have clear lessons for organizations or companies who are faced with institutional complexity as a result of multiple business logics:

- It is not an either-or situation. Traditionally, significant changes in organizational business logics are framed as an out-with-the-old and in-with-the-new situation. It is more effective to try to integrate elements of the new logic while keeping the strong elements of the old logic that made your reputation.

- Stakeholders in the field will tell you what to keep. You cannot ignore your institutional identity. You must pay attention to customers, partners, regulatory agencies and other stakeholders who will define which elements of the old logic are important and need to be maintained.

- Organizational identity aspirations will play a significant role in your response. For all of these business schools, including the elite schools, the intrusion of the IBS logic was seen as an opportunity, not a threat. Responding to new business logics should be guided not by what you are, but by what you aspire to be.

- Status helps guide the details of the response. The scale and format of the changes will depend on your organizational status. ESSEC was already a research-oriented institution; in addition, its Grande École program was so strong that it was able to reposition it as an international MBA. Euromed required a major start-from-scratch overhaul.

REFERENCES
Responding to Institution Complexity: The Role of Identity.
Farah Kodei &, Royston Greenwood. Organization Studies
(January 2014).

Access this and more Ideas at **ideasforleaders.com**

Book Reviews

Deep Purpose

The Heart and Soul of High-Performance Companies

By Ranjay Gulati

Published by Penguin Business, Feb. 2022, 304 pages, ISBN: 978-0241513392

'Purpose isn't a nice-to-have in the business world any longer. It's a must-have." How many times have we heard these words in work conversations? But do these words ring true in your environment or smack of well-meaning yet empty promises to do better in future? We intuitively know that purpose is at the core of what we choose to engage in – the enterprises we help create, the choices we make, what we participate in, through our actions. Yet for many, purpose in its deeper sense, remains elusive. In the words of Paul Polman, former CEO of Unilever, "realising purpose requires both a leadership and systems transformation." Indeed, as this book illustrates, it is a challenge yet also a growth opportunity, well within our reach. The author acknowledges that writing this book was spurred by his belief that "purpose provides new answers to companies and leaders struggling to achieve superior performance amid unforeseen crises and disruptions." He points to short-termism and a performance-at-all-costs mentality that can often lead to unintended consequences and, as we have seen in recent years, with great resignations and the migration of millions of people in the wake of the COVID epidemic, can lead us towards a downward spiral.

Deep Purpose offers a refreshing antithesis to this short-termism. It does so by placing the role of purpose within current and contemporary issues. In a world in transition on many levels, where sustainability remains both paramount and urgent, Gulati argues that the pursuit of profit without purpose is no longer a sustainable business model. He reminds us that purpose cannot be treated separately to the contemporary issues of the day, but rather invites us to bring purpose in – as a foundation to responding well to the world around us.

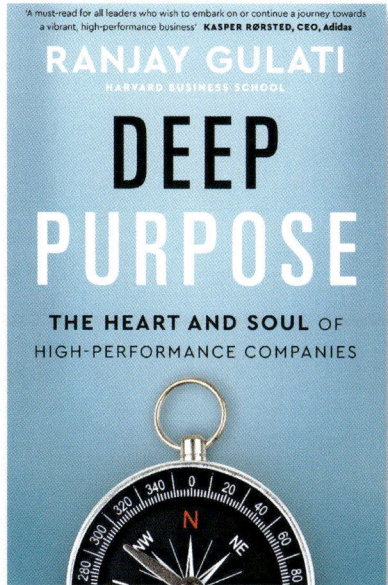

A sense of deep purpose helps to unleash motivation, energy and creativity around us – the bedrocks of innovation and sustainable growth

Many books have been written about the subject of purpose, from enduring religious texts to Victor Frankl's *Man's Search for Meaning*; and more recent additions such as Simon Sinek's *Find Your Why* and others. Our body of knowledge on finding and acting on purpose is formidable. What Ranjay Gulati has attempted to do in *Deep Purpose* is to take us into the minds and hearts of those who are purpose-driven, into the experience of truly purpose-driven organizations, where leadership and systems transformation takes place regularly, being the norm rather than the exception, and to where it pervades beyond an organization's borders into its broader ecosystem.

When practiced well, deep purpose helps us steer our creations in the right direction, navigate uncertainty with more confidence and make wiser and connected choices. A sense of deep purpose helps to unleash motivation, energy and creativity around us – the bedrocks of innovation and sustainable growth.

To help unpack the enormity of the task, the first three chapters focus on how we think about purpose – a much-needed foundation. Chapters 4 to 7 help us explore the actions which leaders can take to define and embed purpose, so that it truly drives performance. These actions include linking purpose to the company's history (a powerful exercise, in my experience), connecting personal and organizational purpose (continually), and injecting more autonomy and collaboration into the organization (and the partnerships and collaborations it forms). In chapter 8, the author highlights several traps that cause purpose to erode over time, something I found particularly useful.

Some readers will find the macro implications of the book most interesting, where purpose is shown to have implications for the future of capitalism. It draws on thought and practice leaders, who have embraced the concept of stakeholder capitalism and developed common metrics to make it a reality. Their journeys not only inspire but open our minds into the practical application of deep purpose, in today's often divisive and uncertain environment.

Other readers might find the book most valuable in its micro implications, as one practices deep purpose in our individual circles of influence and in our personal lives.

What I particularly like about this book is the way it invokes our sense of accountability for striving towards our deep purpose. As leaders, it would be easier to simply seek platitudes for how we make purpose part of everyday language, yet the author sets the bar before us higher. In a gentle yet persistent way, he reminds us that the practice of deep purpose is not separate to thriving as individuals and collectively – the journey towards realizing our deep purpose is an authentic one and words alone won't be sufficient to attain it.

In the author's words, "Deep purpose is an ongoing process to which leaders must commit with all of their heart and soul. It must serve as an operating system for the entire organization as well as a strategic compass for decision-making. A tall order, for sure, but the benefits for stakeholders, for leaders themselves, and for society are enormous."

Jerks at Work

Toxic Co-Workers and What to Do About Them

By Tessa West

Published by Portfolio/Penguin, 2022, ISBN 978-0-5931-9230-6

Despite the business world's HR focus on organizational culture and inclusion, poor interpersonal relations and particularly toxic bosses have a significant negative influence on employee engagement—as exemplified by a recent poll on Monster that revealed 76% of workers currently have or had a toxic manager.

In principle, dealing with bosses who undermine the confidence and mental health of even their best employees, and sanctioning co-workers whose behaviour damages team performance is an organizational issue—one to be delegated to the HR department. Yet in practice there are many reasons HR can't reach in to solve every workplace relationship—a hellish people manager may be indispensable to the company

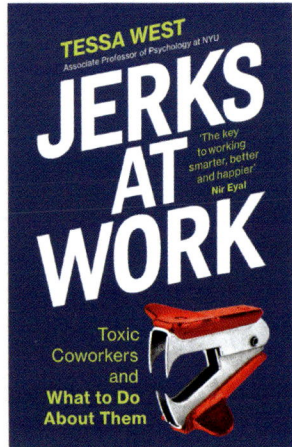

for other reasons; judging a co-worker to be antisocial can be very subjective.

Consequently, in most cases, individual workers need to overcome bad situations created by jerks at work, by themselves—which is where this new book comes in.

Author Tessa West, Associate Professor of Psychology at New York University, is a leading expert on interpersonal interaction and communication. She has a good sense of humour and a rich fund of workplace anecdotes, which she deploys along with numerous psychological insights to make this both a very useful handbook and a fun read. Jerks at Work: Toxic Co-Workers and What to Do About Them, not only has an irresistible title—who hasn't been demotivated by 'bad apple' colleagues or nasty bosses—but also delivers what the sub-title suggests.

Drawing on a decade of research into classic workplace archetypes, West presents a rogues' gallery of problem people—including the Gas-lighter, the Bulldozer, the Credit-stealer, the Neglecter, the Free-rider, and the Micromanager—revealing the motivations and insecurities that lie behind their bad behaviour and offering psychologically savvy ways to deal with each type of jerk. That can be 'deal' in not letting them negatively affect your life/work, or in some cases helping jerks at work to change their ways.

Work places can be highly competitive. People who might appear well adjusted and empathetic in their private lives can find the stress of work and the need to succeed in high-pressured environments tips them into jerk-at-work behaviours—causing stress and anxiety for co-workers and ultimately

West presents a rogues' gallery of problem people—including the Gas-lighter, the Bulldozer, the Credit-stealer, the Neglecter, the Free-rider, and the Micromanager

interfering with team performance. This can be an HR issue but in the first instance being armed with the strategies West recommends can be invaluable.

As an appendix the book offers two quizzes: i) Am I a Jerk at Work? ii) Am I an Effective Ally? Your reviewer, I am relieved to say, passed in both cases—though perhaps not with the flying colours he had arrogantly assumed. In fact, these quizzes are a very clever way of pinpointing the complex issues involved and explaining how to address them.

West concludes with the story of the NASA engineers who put the Perseverance rover on Mars. Bringing together multiple disciplines and working together for three years, the team knew there would be arguments, but also knew there was absolutely no room for sustained conflict.

The strategies they used to resolve potential problems echo West's advice. For example, when reporting on progress they realized their constant use of 'we', which they had thought to be fair, was not authentic. It was more important, having monitored individual contributions, to acknowledge personal credit—a typical case where the way to resolve conflict is not always obvious and where West's book offers some unique insight.

The Necessary Journey

Making Real Progress on Equity and Inclusion

By Ella F. Washington

Published by Harvard Business Review Press, 2022, ISBN 978-1-64782-128-9

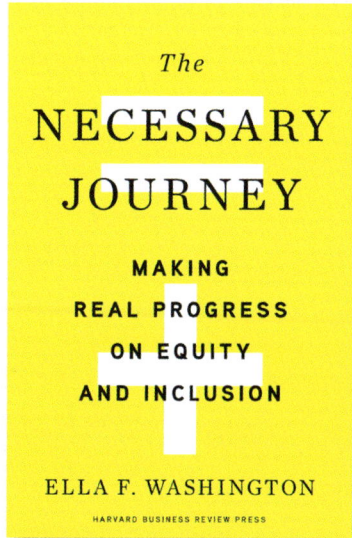

Shortly after George Floyd's murder, Dr. Ella Washington co-authored an article for the Harvard Business Review titled: "U.S. Businesses Must Take Meaningful Action Against Racism." This is now the context that sets the tone for her new book.

However, The Necessary Journey: Making Real Progress on Equity and Inclusion is far more than a polemic against racism. Rather it is a deep exploration of the journey, stage-by-stage, that a range of well-known companies have taken towards achieving significant and sustainable diversity, equity and inclusion (DEI) goals.

As such it offers valuable guidance and motivation for any organization committed to creating an inclusive environment

DEI done right can create great places to work, improve employees' wellbeing and performance, and provide access to untapped talent

where all employees can thrive on equal terms—to their and the organization's mutual benefit.

While racial equality, gender diversity and social justice generally should be corporate priorities, it is important that they are not viewed by business leaders as part of some vague utopian vision—consequently relegated to boxes to be ticked or even ignored in a backlash.

It is essential that the business-positive, performance enhancing aspects of DEI are emphasized—and seen as a key part of the prize at the end of the journey. DEI done right can create great places to work, improve employees' wellbeing and performance, provide access to untapped talent, bring the company closer to its customer base, and greatly enrich the organization's capacity for diverse critical thinking and innovation.

Dr. Ella F. Washington is an organizational psychologist, founder of the DEI consultancy Ellavate Solutions, and Professor of Practice at Georgetown University's McDonough School of Business. As a black woman who has worked for many years in the corporate world, she is only too aware of the barriers to DEI, not to mention the outright racism, sexism and homophobia that exists in places. But she has seen significant progress over the years and is optimistic about the future.

The core message of her book is that the journey from good intentions to truly establishing a diverse and inclusive workplace with a mature DEI culture is hard, requiring invention and reinvention, trial and error, humility, adaption to a changing world, constant rethinking, and some trade-offs and sacrifices. A difficult but always a necessary journey—for which Washington provides a simple map. Each journey is divided into these five stages:

1. **Awareness**: realizing why DEI matters to the organization
2. **Compliance**: meeting legal requirements and doing DEI "because we have to"
3. **Tactical**: fitting DEI into overall company goals
4. **Integration**: creating alignment between DEI efforts externally (brand image) and internally (employee reality). This is notoriously where Nike got it wrong
5. **Sustainability**: DEI systems and culture that can survive business cycles, strategy changes, and changes of leadership.

The majority of the book is taken up by nine chapters—narratives of the DEI journey taken by nine individual companies. The leaders of these companies, which include Best Buy, Infosys, PwC, Slack, and Sodexo, share their experiences with Washington, detailing their successes, failures and lessons learned at the five different stages. These unique mini case studies provide practical guidance for other business leaders, either planning to take this essential journey, or more likely as a way to benchmark what progress they have currently made.

Power and Prediction

The Disruptive Economics of Artificial Intelligence

By Ajay Agrawal, Joshua Gans, and Avi Goldfarb

Published by Harvard Business Review Press, 2022, ISBN 978-1-6478-2419-8

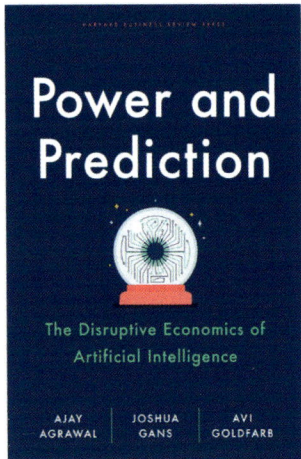

I n their influential 2018 book, 'Prediction Machines', the authors of this new book sought to dispel the myth and hype around AI by reframing its power and potential as being a drop in the cost of making predictions. Cheaper prediction-making leading to improved decision-making.

This insight clarified the economic effect of AI in a business context and provided a basis for executives and entrepreneurs to focus strategic action. In an era of extreme uncertainty this was and is important. Uncertainty hampers decision-making and holds back strategy. A better, faster, access to reliable predictions can unblock this, easing decision-making, and creating opportunities for business growth.

In their new book, 'Power and Prediction', Ajay Agrawal, Joshua Gans, and Avi Goldfarb, eminent economists from Rotman School of Management, address gaps in their original thinking. And offer new insights that have been revealed as more and more organizations have adopted AI technologies across different industries. In considering the economics of AI, rather than focusing as they had on the manifest capabilities of AI technology itself, the authors realized they should pay more attention to context—the varied systems in which AI operates or might potentially operate and the economic forces on them.

While it remains true that AI creates value through improved decision-making, it has become clear that effective AI adoption and real transformation is dependent on the creation of new systems driven by the technology. This became apparent because many nimble small companies, as well as larger companies already well staffed with data scientists, quickly adopted AI solutions, whereas other organizations that could benefit from AI were very slow to adopt. The sluggishness being largely due to these organizations being constrained by their existing rules and systems, which made them resistant to the changes successful AI adoption typically entails.

For example, in the case of innovation productivity, where AI can help move from reliance on trial and error to fast and credible hypothesis generation, progress is only made if the next steps in the process are redesigned to allow for this new-found efficiency—otherwise it will just lead to a bottleneck of untested, undeveloped ideas, rather than clear decision taking. The entire innovation system needs to be redesigned.

Decision-making, the authors remind us, involves prediction and judgment—an instinctive two-part mental process we don't always differentiate. Machine learning and AI technologies shift the prediction part from humans to machines, increasing the speed and accuracy of predictions. For the judgement part to keep pace organizations need to create or redesign their systems. Redesigning systems of interdependent decisions takes time, and for many industries the authors say we are at a "between time"—but "when these new systems emerge, they can be disruptive on a global scale."

'Power and Prediction' offers an invaluable guide to these complex developments—helping companies navigate what is likely to be a profound change, that for most will be unavoidable if they want to stay competitive. While highlighting the opportunities and economic benefits, the book also addresses some of the threats and barriers to AI fulfilling its potential in organizations. The authors introduce several concepts that need to be considered, such as:

The Between Times. The current uncertain start to AI adoption, due to a lack of appreciation of the effect of the larger systems in which AI operates, will pass and adoption will accelerate. Some will be left behind.

The AI Bullwhip. Small changes in one area, brought by AI driven decisions, may reverberate through a system and lead to unintended consequences and possible cracks elsewhere.

Power and Disruption. AI only has power as it leads to better decisions. Humans still control decision-making and it is wrong to think that AI per se holds any power. Value creation depends on organizations changing so that humans and machines can work together well.

Bias and Discrimination. It is often suggested that AI can perpetuate bias. The authors argue that AI can detect bias and adjust for it. However, this requires overcoming challenges around regulations designed for the pre-AI era and resisting external pressure for bias.

About the Publishers

Ideas for Leaders

Ideas for Leaders summarizes the thinking of the foremost researchers and experts on leadership and management practice from the world's top business schools and management research institutions. With these concise and easily readable 'Ideas' you can quickly and easily inform yourself and your colleagues about the latest insights into management best practice.

The research-based Ideas are supported by a growing series of podcasts with influential thinkers, CEOs, and other leading leadership and management experts from large organizations and small. We also publish book reviews and a new series of online programs.

www.ideasforleaders.com

The Center for the Future of Organization (CFFO)

CFFO is an independent Think Tank and Research Center at the Drucker School of Management at Claremont Graduate University. The Center's mission is to deepen our understanding of new capabilities that are critical to succeed in a digitally connected world, and to support leaders and organizations along their transformational journey.

In the tradition of Peter Drucker, the Center works across disciplines, combining conceptual depth with practical applicability and ethical responsibility, in close collaboration and connection with thought leaders and practice leaders from academia, business, and consulting.

www.futureorg.org